BIRD OF JOVE

NUMBER SEVENTEEN:

Louise Lindsey Merrick Natural Environment Series

BIRD OF JOVE

BY DAVID BRUCE

Texas A&M University Press

College Station

This edition published by arrangement with G. P. Putnam's Sons
First Texas A&M University Press printing: March, 1994

The paper used in this book meets the minimum requirements
of the American National Standard for Permanence
of Paper for Printed Library Materials, Z39.48-1984.
Binding materials have been chosen for durability.

Library of Congress Cataloging-in-Publication Data

Bruce, David.
        Bird of Jove / David Bruce.
                p.   cm.
        Originally published: New York : Putnam, 1971.
        ISBN 0-89096-604-4 (pbk.)
        1. Himalayan golden eagle. 2. Falconry. 3. Barnes, Sam.
I. Title.
[QL696.F32B78   1994]
598.9'16–dc20   93-21439
                                                        CIP

To Mary Patchett
author and friend, without whose help
in the preparation of this manuscript this book
could not have been published
—Sam Barnes

ILLUSTRATIONS

PROLOGUE

The Berkut, largest and fiercest species of the golden eagle, supremely merits the description by Shakespeare, Wordsworth and other writers, "Bird of Jove"—an allusion to the legend of those eagles belonging to the Roman god Jove (Jupiter) which were said to have thunderbolts in their talons because of the manner in which they took their prey.

IN the remote Kirghiz Republic of the Soviet Union there is a lake known as Issyk-Kul, whose brackish waters extend for a hundred and fifteen miles at more than five thousand feet above sea level. The lake's surface is shadowed by the Tien Shan, Mountains of the Gods, rising to a majestic peak of twenty thousand feet.

To the northeast, Russian settlers cultivate rice, silkworms, and the sinister opium poppy. The pale wintry sky looks down on lesser ranges, on peaks and snow-carpeted uplands where sky-blue forget-me-nots are trodden underfoot by bahrial, antelope, and the fiercely beautiful snow leopards. Here, a survival of the Ice Age, the Tien Shan snow hare races his zigzag course on fluffy, snowshoe hind feet. These hares are never killed by the local people, who tell you that they are the souls of frightened children and that they cry like babies before they die.

Streams find their way down the mountain slopes into Issyk-Kul, and trees grow in the valleys made by them; the old Silk Road winds along the shore, where reed-covered marshes are haunted by boar and tiger. The tops of the pines are sometimes swathed in mist as the moisture condenses in the morning air. It is said that Pudna, the sacred lotus, grows there, bearing the legendary seeds of forgetfulness that stole the memory of Penelope from Ulysses.

There, in round felt tents called kurts, live nomad herdsmen who breed fat-tailed sheep, small shaggy ponies, and the double-humped Bactrian camels. They pasture their flocks on the high, alpine meadows in the summer and in the winter move down into the valleys. These dark men of Kara-Kirghiz origin sometimes throw back to the straight-nosed, blue-eyed Uzans of Central Asia, who were driven westward by the Huns in the second century.

Not a gentle landscape, but a noble one with a clear, Spartan beauty of its own. Here, high against the sky, over mountain and valley, above the long strip of shining water, spirals a living creature infinitely more beautiful than them all, the golden eagle that was to become Atalanta. She is a Berkut, the royal eagle of the Tartars. In the great days of falconry her kind was flown only by an emperor. She is a hunter of wolves, of bears and tigers, deer and foxes, capable of stooping on her prey at more than a hundred and twenty miles an hour.

This is the world of lake and mountain into which Atalanta was born. Above her nest in an alpine crevice she heard the singing wings of migrating swans pass overhead; when a vixen screamed below, Atalanta's "kek kek kek" mingled with the other wild sounds. It was on these mountain slopes that her master, Sam Barnes, found her, and here that he almost lost her again.

Much later, Atalanta came to know the smaller but no less beautiful world of Snowdonia, a rugged region between Anglesea and Cardigan Bay. The Welsh, poets of folklore, call Snowdon Caer Eryri, "Camp of the Eagles." Though not comparable in height to the peaks overshadowing Issyk-Kul, Snowdon is nevertheless a giant in its own domain. They say that when storms thunder over Snowdon it is the beating of a multitude of wings that you hear; birds are gathering about a royal golden eagle and the Celts say, "they are breeding whirlwinds."

In Wales there are spare, masculine mountains divided again and again by paths of crystal descending to fill swift-flowing streams close-hidden under dark foliage. Today this is Atalanta's world. She has bridged these strangely similar, yet so disparate, worlds through her master, a tall, sinewy Lancashireman, with an unruly head of blond hair and the puckish look of a Danny Kaye. He is Sam Barnes of Pwllheli, a fine naturalist, an athlete, and an outstanding falconer.

There was a long delay before Sam added another chapter to Atalanta's life. Many obstacles had to be overcome before she could be manned (handled) again and allowed to enter the game that is her heritage—flying free over snowy peaks, hearing the vixen's eerie cry, and chasing the red banner of a running fox—and return, at his call, to the fist of the man who loves her and to the inseparable companionship of Shep, the great Welsh sheep dog who is her playmate and hunting companion, and who, too, is so much a part of her story.

Atalanta
© *John D. Drysdale*

ONE

The true falconer must at all times be patient
. . . he must realize that he is under an im-
mense obligation to his hawk. Whatever he
wants to do, his hawk must be his first con-
sideration, the ruling factor of his life.

—SAM BARNES

SAM BARNES first saw his eagle from the high, mountain-ous slopes of the Tien Shan above Issyk-Kul Lake in the Kirghiz Republic. High in the cold, clear air she turned her head and the feathers on her neck shone like gold. She was, as Shakespeare once called her kind, "gorgeous as the sun at midsummer."

This beautiful bird was one of the great Asian Berkuts, the eagles of the emperors. No other man was allowed to fly them under pain of death; they were the hunters of Gen-ghis Khan, of Saladin, and of the czars. They took the biggest game—wolves, antelopes, foxes, bears, and a cast (two) of them flew against leopards and tigers. They beat their wings about the heads of furiously galloping wild horses to slow them until their Mongol masters could capture them.

Sam Barnes, naturalist and supreme falconer, is also a gambler and an adventurer, an ardent ornithologist, and an authority on everything connected with hunting birds. He went to Berlin to pursue his studies and was admitted into the Eastern sector to study in the museums. This led to his being asked to join a scientific expedition interested in the flora and fauna of Kirghizstan, home of the great wolf-killing Berkut, the most ferocious species of the golden eagle.

Sam left with the expedition, determineed by hook or by crook to bring back a Berkut. It is said that Westerners can never train them, but Sam did not believe this. He had traiñed eagles, falcons, short-winged hawks, and other birds said to be untrainable; now he wanted to try his skill on a Berkut.

The expedition got underway and the scientists were camped high on the Tien Shan, when Sam became separated from his companions. He had collected plants and taken natural history notes and had decided to do some exploring on his own. After a stiff climb he found himself looking down at the settlement of some Kirghiz tribesmen —athletic mountaineers with Mongol features, living as their ancestors had lived for centuries.

Set up in a circle on a flattened piece of mountainside were the black felt kurts of the tribesmen. The tents were familiar enough to Sam, but not the sight inside the circle. There, short-tied to a branch to weather were five great hunting Berkuts. The huge birds were immobile under the cold rays of the sun that glinted off their copper feathering, powerful killers all and menacing in their immobility. Sam guessed their eyelids were seeled, sewn together in the cruel fashion of their primitive masters, so that they can the better manage the hunters they consider untamable. Only at the moment their prey appears are their eyelids unseeled.

Sam strode down to the settlement, where a small smiling man led him to Khan Chalsan's kurt. Chalsan was tough and muscular, heavily robed, and armed with a hunting knife thrust through his belt. He spoke fair English and some German, so Sam had little difficulty understanding him. He followed his host into the kurt and a round of courtesies began.

All during the brandy and small talk Sam concealed his impatience to see the Berkuts at close quarters, for he knew he must wait until all the preliminaries were over. When he finally got around to telling Chalsan of his interest in the eagles, Chalsan informed him they were kept for hunting wolves in this icy place where a gunshot might start an avalanche. They were chained killers, living in a state of near starvation, condemned to a life of viciousness through hunger; they would never be companions to their masters, these mighty hunters that, with a trained dog, could bring down leopards and tigers.

"Your eagles are just chained killers," Sam said impatiently. "If I had one I'd keep it the way you keep your Chinese hawk eagle." And he pointed to where the Khan's favorite Chinese hawk eagle brooded contentedly on its perch.

The Khan smiled. "You could not, Sahib. Those Berkuts

go two or three weeks without food and they hunt only to eat. For centuries my people have trained them to this. It is an ancient tradition and we are proud of our mighty killers and use them only for hunting." He rose. "But come and see for yourself."

Sam followed his host out of the kurt to where the Berkuts were tied. Sam would not be the falconer he is if he allowed fear to affect him. Leaning forward, he took the Khan's glove and then took the eagle up on his left fist and felt its weight; he moved his fist so that the Berkut opened its wings to balance itself, and he rejoiced in the great span. He held the leash in his free hand as he looked down at the powerful feet. He drew it idly across them.

The Berkut tensed its grip and tears of agony came into Sam's eyes. Later he learned that the Berkuts were fed while hooded, and that the signal for feeding was to trail the leash across their talons. To the eagle, Sam's fingers were food for its starved body, and no man could break its grip. The Khan removed the hood and then unseeled its lids. It raised its hackles and increased its paralyzing grip.

From his robes the Khan produced a large piece of raw meat which he dangled before the eagle. It snatched the meat with its free, steel-tipped talons, and in the diversion Sam freed his fist from its talons.

As Sam massaged his fingers, Chalsan explained that he gave his Berkuts big bones with little meat on them because, in the mountains, Berkuts do not die of age, they starve to death when the top mandible grows around the bottom one so that the eagle cannot feed.

Although Sam was thrilled by the great birds, he was also

horrified by the way they were treated. "If I owned a Berkut," he told the Khan, "I would man it too well for it to need a hood or to have its eyelids seeled. I would keep it with me always and disregard the practice in falconry of starving a bird into obedience. My eagle would fly because it loved me, not to get food," he went on heatedly. "It's immoral for those hunger-crazed eagles of yours to fly low and straight for short distances and then to kill like crazy lunatics. That is not a pleasing spectacle."

Chalsan smiled coldly. He said that the hunting Berkuts killed wolves during the lifetimes of several masters. "A trained Berkut is worth a dozen young and lively wives and more than twenty Bactrian camels. For you a Berkut would be priceless and you can never own one."

Obviously the subject had been dismissed, and for the rest of his stay Sam became silently observant. Hunting with the Khan, Sam saw the great Berkut flown at the beautiful Tien Shan snow hare, whose ancestry goes back through a world of icy tundras and beyond to the Ice Age itself; a hare whose red blood makes it valuable to predators in that cruelly cold region.

It was autumn. Sam and the Khan camped near Issyk-Kul, fifteen thousand feet up in the mountains. It was a time when birds migrated in their thousands to warmer territories and the humans traveled through the Northwest Frontier to the Peshawar Valley to hire themselves out as labor during the hard winter months, returning to their mountain homes and their flocks of sheep and goats in spring—following the custom of centuries.

When the Khan released the Berkut and flew it at the

first snow hare Sam had seen, he felt a deep sadness. The hare's fur was whiter than the snow around it, and it ran zigzag fashion. Like all hares it was faster uphill, and it made prodigious sideways leaps. Sam pleaded with Chalsan to hold the eagle until the hare was safe. He could not bear a creature of such beauty to be destroyed. The Berkut shook and panted and struggled to leave Chalsan's fist.

Sometimes the hare broke the continuity of its descent by leaping from one rock to another for more than twenty feet. Chalsan tightened his grip on the eagle in line with Sam's wish, but his grip was not tight enough—the Berkut jerked her foot free and was away, going down the slope with her heavy, powerful wingbeats. She gained momentum and banked round into the wind so that her speed shot her up to a hundred feet or more. As she turned she came with the wind at an incredible pace designed to retain her height, but even with that impetus she had dropped to fifty feet halfway to the hare.

An inner sense warned the graceful, gentle hare of approaching doom. She stopped her sideways leaping maneuver, breaking her scent, and thrust her ears erect. Then she scudded at breakneck speed up the slope toward a birch tree and safety. Her survival weapons were her acute hearing and her speed, and she bounded along in ten-foot stretches. The eagle had three times the speed of the hare. The hare becomes a sitting target as she rises, ears pricked, nose twitching, trying to pinpoint the danger. That is when the "sportsman" gets his shot in, and the hare dies, screaming like a bewildered child.

This stop to assess its danger is an inbred habit with the

hare, and it was the undoing of the Berkut's prey. The hare stopped, her back to the wind, panting as she rose erect to get a better view. The eagle came in over her, fast and low. The timid creature squatted, using the camouflage of the snow. She stayed motionless with her ears back. In this position, with the hare quite static, humans have been known to step on one.

But the eagle's sight was too keen. She banked into the wind, sweeping along near the ground, her strong legs extended before her, and came at the hare head on. As she pounced, the hare made a wild jump. The Berkut exploded into activity. She spread her tail, backpedaled her outstretched wings, using the force of the wind as a brake. As the hare shot up, the eagle caught her in midair, catching the lovely animal as carelessly as a boy catches a thrown snowball, and brought the limp body down to the snow.

Sam had much to learn, and his interest pleased Chalsan. He stayed some time in the settlement and he and the Khan climbed the perilous slopes on their sturdy yaks. When they could ride no higher, the men continued on foot to reach a Berkut's nest high on the ledge.

They crossed the ice field leading to the last steep climb in this world of the eagles. It was a day when thermal currents made whirlwinds spring up and move along the massive ice field. These are whirling columns of snow that pick up everything in their paths and grow larger and larger as they stride fiercely into the distance. The sun glances off them until they seem like walking rainbows, and other columns shine with the fire of burnished copper. While they rage, their power could tear and destroy life, but their life cycle is short, and when it is over they dissolve into very ordinary cumulus clouds.

The cliff face was framed by the mountain, and the men were above it, making the final approach down a belt of moving scree, using the giant footsteps of practiced mountaineers on the sliding scree and landing safely on the rimrock, ready to rest after their effort.

Sam remembered the cry of "Look to the left, Sahib," and saw again the black patch of dark Caucasian firs standing straight on the precipitous side of the mountain. Below them a herd of deer bounded along a narrow path, trying to reach the cover of the firs. Then he saw the reason for their alarm.

Against the hard sky two Berkuts and one Steller's sea eagle were dive-bombing the herd. A hind dropped out of the race to protect her young one, and the female Berkut dropped from the sky onto the hind's back. The cruel talons bit deeper, and the hind fell while the young one fled in terror.

It was the little deer the great birds wanted. Releasing the hind, the female Berkut flew lazily after the prey, and the two killers followed the terrified youngster. The male Berkut was over the little deer, but he had to fly a zigzag course along the winding path. The male flew low and positioned itself to drop as the small deer ran alongside a big rock. The Berkut's great legs reached out to kill—when its right wing smacked against the rock and almost toppled it over the precipice. It came back to the attack from the side.

The baby deer stopped seconds away from death, almost paralyzed by fear. Even so, it came to sudden life and bolted into a narrow crevice between the rocks and went to ground. The male Berkut, with its six-foot wingspan, could not fly in the narrow space, so it landed, barking with anger and frustration and using its tail as a springboard as it flapped its wings and sprang up and down, stabbing into the narrow darkness with its steel-shod talons. The yelping sea eagle landed.

Sam breathed a sigh of relief as the deer remained panting and quivering, pressed close to the ground, but Chalsan smiled. "Watch the female Berkut, Sahib. She has two hungry nestlings to feed and will not give up easily."

Sam peered to where the female soared on outstretched wings two hundred feet above. Intelligent eagle that she was, she did not repeat the male's mistake. Through his binoculars Sam saw her high above, gliding sideways on a strong headwind with hardly a wingbeat and at tremendous speed. She flew straight and true and commenced her stoop with taut, arched wings. The gravitational pull on her twenty pounds plus of body enabled her to reach a great speed, and the herd of running deer beneath her seemed to be standing still.

Selecting the deer nearest the edge of the precipice, she stooped, a true bird of Jove, carrying thunderbolts in her talons. She struck, driving these talons into the deer's back, maddening it with fear and pain so that it jumped over the precipice and fell to its death on the rocks below. The young eagles would be fed.

Yet the female did not fly down to the kill. She left that to her mate and to the sea eagle. These great birds would eat, then dissect the deer, carrying the best pieces to their nests. In the recognized order of feeding, the vultures would not move in until the eagles left. The vultures had neither the feet for carrying nor the beaks for dissecting fresh game, permitting them to reach the soft entrails. Without the eagles they would have had to wait until the body putrified.

The splendid female Berkut rose to an immense height where, moving her wings at intervals, she could hover and command a view of her surroundings. The Khan said, "She has gone into the sun, Sahib, because she can see something that we cannot."

Indeed she had seen something. As she stooped on her new prey, a bar-headed goose, first cousin to the giant gray-lag, weighing twelve pounds and breeding only in the Himalayas, Sam, watching her pluck the goose out of the air, knew he was seeing a hunting bird for which he would trade everything he had.

Sam turned impulsively toward Chalsan, so excited by what he had seen that he forgot he was talking to a man to whom bargaining was the breath of life.

"I'd give everything I have for that eagle!"

The Khan shook his head. "That eagle you admire so much will soon die, and no one can save her. That's why I allowed you to see her. She has the white death. I set her free to breed; in captivity she would have died long ago. There is no cure for her."

Sam was shocked. "But she flies magnificently—it doesn't make sense."

"The white death is incurable. We call it that because something like a creamy kumiss grows around inside her throat and under her tongue. As it grows it thickens and in the end it will choke her."

Sam yearned to pinpoint the disease. "Tell me," he said, "did you feed her pigeons when she was in training?"

Chalsan was puzzled. "She ate many pigeons. She is too heavy to carry on the fist, so I carried her on a pole between two ponies. This mighty hunter last winter killed a black wolf, and she fought me all the time with her talons—"

Sam interrupted him, "Did she eat the whole pigeon?"

"She plucked and ate the pigeons I gave her," the Khan said.

"Then I believe she has what we call frounce, the type brought by pigeons, called pigeon canker. It is transmitted by a tiny parasite. I'm so afraid of the disease that I never feed even healthy pigeons to a bird of prey until they have been dead at least a day because cold kills the virus. I want to go near your bird, I want to see her feed."

The men followed the rimrock to the rockfall at the end of the sheer cliff face, and then they went down and followed the contour of the cliff. They were mountain men and jumped from one scarcely visible foothold to another. Trees grew straight from the sparse soil, and there was a musty smell from the dank loam and rotting growth, a peculiar but not unpleasant odor.

Four hundred feet down they came on an open area of grass and alpine plants growing on a wide ledge along the cliff face. The men took a precarious path along the narrowed ledge, pressed against the cliff wall. Sam heard the Khan whisper, "The nest is on the shelf beneath the overhang, that is why we could not see it from below."

The ledge gave way to a sloping, grassy shelf jutting out over empty air. They rested, and Sam saw the great bird's nest built into a small grassy cavity halfway along the ledge beneath the overhang. This protected the baby eagles from the sun, for the direct rays would kill them. At the end of the ledge a dark cave was crowned by a grassy plateau; on it the Berkut mantled and plucked at the goose she had killed. Around her on the grass were the remains of squirrels, hares, rabbits, and other prey. This meant that the young were now tearing at their own meat; they needed a variety of foods and a constant supply of fur, feathers, and bones with their fresh meat to make the castings that clean their internal track.

Sam, sweeping his binoculars wide, picked up the male Berkut sailing on motionless wings surveying the two men —and not liking what it saw. It rose in ever-widening circles, sometimes with its wings motionless and sometimes with rapid wingbeats. As it rose, this robber of the mountains and valleys, it sent its yelping cry of defiance at the intruders, and the cry echoed and bounced from the cliff face. The sun touched the male's richly dark plumage and its white wing and tail patches and turned to gold the wing coverts and the burnished head and hackles. The eagle stood out in bold relief against a patch of blue sky, then it disappeared over the white-capped ridges.

There were two young eagles in the nest. They had reached the stage at which they should fly, and yet Sam was puzzled to see they were not flying. He was also surprised to find two youngsters in the nest; generally the only survivor is the female, which, as with all birds of prey, is the largest.

After a few days' growth, she will tear up her brother along with her own food.

As the two men approached the bulky nest, the young eagles retreated to the rear, but without greatly resenting the intruders, merely opening and snapping their beaks. The foundations of the nest were branches, some of them as thick as a man's forearm, and the bowl was padded with roots, grass, and bracken. The center cradle was lined with dried fern fronds, moss, grass, and tufts of green herbage; and around the rim were placed green pine branches.

Chalsan threw the female a piece of meat and she danced about and played with it before she swallowed it.

Chalsan laughed with pleasure and boasted, "She will make a mighty hunter, Sahib!"

Sam shook his head, "No, she will not. She will not be able to fly until she moults and her primaries are clipped. She won't live through the winter here when her mother cannot feed her and she is unable to fly herself."

"Never fear, Sahib. Every two days a shepherd boy will come here and take the food brought by the old ones. The boy and his family live on the game the parent eagles bring, and in exchange he will leave soft red meat for the young."

Sam was appalled. "You mean you retard the young eagles' flight to force their parents to feed them beyond the usual time?"

"Yes Sahib, and we eat good! Geese, partridge, ptarmigan, hare, rabbit, and we leave ewe meat in exchange."

Chalsan disregarded Sam's disapproving grunt. "We take the young eagles with us when we leave for the winter and feed them well for three or four years until their white tails

Sam first saw his eagle in the remote Kirghiz Republic of the Soviet Union
© *S. Barnes*

An eagle's sight is twelve times sharper than man's

have gone. We only train them from November to March, and we feed them as much as they can eat for the rest of the year. Then we set the finest ones free to hunt and breed and take them up again at seven or eight years for full-time hunting, winter and summer. This way they grow and yet keep their wild instincts, and they are not too afraid of man."

Sam was silent, thinking how young eagles and falcons in the West are taken straight from the nest for training and how many keep their nestling hunger call which spoils them for hunting. No Kirghiz tribesman would dare to own such a "screamer."

He tried to explain the very different Western approach to training. Chalsan listened, nodding but not really understanding the emotional dislike of civilized man to inflicting pain. Sam plowed on, telling him that an eagle must be fed to get into hunting trim so that it attains the same condition as when it hunts in the wild; when it is "sharp set," eager to hunt, it is keen and lively; exceed this and the bird becomes lazy. At its standard hunting weight it is at its best, but it is also near death. If a careless falconer forgets several feeds, the healthy-looking eagle simply topples over or goes into a fit that will be fatal when it is caused by starvation.

The well-nourished eagle can live on its two layers of fat for as long as three weeks. Only when this fat is burned away will it be in full yarak, at the top of its form. It is not only cruel but it is also stupid to train a first-year eagle to hunt, for its temper is easily ruined and it has no scope for its natural playfulness; also it will never gain its full powers of flight.

But in spite of his Western beliefs, Sam respected Chalsan, a man who had traveled widely and a wise man in his way. "Our Berkuts are sacred to us," Chalsan replied. "In the days when falconry flourished in Europe, they were sometimes given to a king as our most highly prized gift. I've told you today's price to a berkutschi, a man who hunts with his Berkuts, in wives and camels. Our Mongol emperors flew Berkuts; Genghis Khan and Kublai Khan flew them against the largest prey. Our eagles hunt in the bleak uplands of Tibet; they kill deer in Chinese Tartary and wolves on our wild Kirghiz steppes. They can live and hunt in any type of country; no bird compares with them. We believe they transfer some of their magic to their owners. They are the most treasured possession of any hunter lucky enough to own one. Our Berkuts are the largest and the best hunting eagles in the world. They breed here on the Tien Shan rock face and they have been bred for size, power, and courage for centuries."

Chalsan pointed skyward at the massive form of the female eagle hovering above them. "That female above us killed a giant crane when she was a youngster and smaller than her prey. She is a haggard (moulted in the wild) and she has reared her two young in freedom. It is no mean thing to be a wolf-killer in these mountains. She flies at wolves because they are the first thing she sees when she is unhooded. When she is free in the wild she will only fly at a wolf through necessity or when other game is scarce. Our wolves often weigh over ten stone. Wrongly taken, they can kill an eagle or badly damage it before the bird can get its death grip. I have myself seen a wolf kill three Berkuts before it was killed by the fourth. A Berkut must fly in the right wind and be taught to take the wolf through the head after blinding it with blows from its wings. Badly taken, the wolf can tear the eagle's wings or splinter its legs. She, that one up there, killed a lone black wolf preying on our sheep and goats. Now she must die herself of the creeping white death. But she will live again in her daughter, who will become a mighty hunter like her doomed mother."

Sam looked upward. "She is magnificent," he agreed.

"She is not yet five years old. Her plumage is still immature. We set her free early to keep her alive, and luckily she bred young."

The eagle seemed to hang in space, her eyes piercing the sky. Of all birds, eagles have the most powerful sight—twelve times sharper than man's.

At that moment, high in the Mountains of the Gods, Sam made up his mind that he could be satisfied with nothing less than the glorious creature flying above him; if he must he would lie, cheat, do anything to possess her. And he would cure her terrible disease.

They returned to the kurts, and Sam took his leave and went with the tribesman who had days before located the scientific expedition. His friends welcomed him with an understanding of his driving need to possess the great bird. Meantime he collected specimens of mountain plants, observed the life of the snows, and always kept in touch with his friend, the Khan Chalsan.

In this way Sam learned that Chalsan had reclaimed the now greatly weakened eagle. This was what he had been waiting for; his chance had come. He traveled to the craggy wilderness of the lower slope where the Khan and his people, his flocks, and the great eagle had moved to their winter settlement.

Sam bent his fair head and pushed past the thick folds at the entrance to Chalsan's kurt. Through the inner gloom he could see the great eagle on a cross-perch. It took no experience to see that she was a very sick bird. Sam had brought with him a large supply of the Khan's beloved brandy and cigarettes. They sat down and hospitality began. Chalsan noticed the direction in which Sam's eyes were straying.

"She is very near death, Sahib," he said sadly.

Sam did not dispute this. Unless her death was a certainty in the Khan's mind, his plan would fail. He waited, and when the time seemed ripe he made his offer.

"Chalsan, the great eagle is dying. It would bring me great happiness to own her even for the few weeks of life that are left—"

"We do not trade our Berkuts with Westerners."

Sam was silent, knowing that the shrewd trader in Chalsan was weighing up these few weeks of life against the curious streak of sentimentality he knew to be a part of Westerners. Chalsan made up his mind; he would have the best of the bargain.

"Very well, if you want her so much, she is yours."

The exchange was made and Sam left that day, taking his dying eagle with him. Time was short. Sam rode, walked, and luckily was able to get a lift by air. He knew that in Kabul he would be able to get help for his eagle at the medical institute. It was her only chance. Frounce, a disease of the mouth and tongue, was spreading down the bird's throat. Sam treated her to keep her from choking, by burning her throat with a silver nitrate stick and cleaning it with gentian violet, nourishing the bird by blowing chicken blood and egg yolk into her crop through a glass pipette. This care kept her alive until an American drug, entramin, arrived. With dramatic suddenness, the cure took place in about seven days.

The eagle recovered her strength, and when she was well enough they set out on the journey back to Wales. Then, at the East-West German border, Sam was told he would be allowed to pass through but his eagle would not; she would be destroyed. Sam offered all he had for permission to take her with him. He was refused. His eagle must die.

He was stunned by the unexpectedness of the ruling. With still a few hours before he must board the train, Sam turned away, sick at heart. All he could feel through his numbness was the gentle pressure of the talons of the great bird on his arm. She had come back to splendid life—only to be condemned at the height of her splendor.

As he stood in the bleak border railway station holding the great copper eagle that was the fulfillment of his life-long dream, he knew a feeling known only to the falconers of old—the deep emotional bond that can exist between a man and his hawk.

Because inaction was impossible, Sam walked quickly in an effort not to think, and after a time he found himself beside a fence beyond which were animal cages.

When a man is without hope he clutches at any straw. The cages told him that there must be someone there who cared about animals. He opened the gate and went inside.

In one enclosure was the shaggy shape of a wolf, peering through the bars with narrowed eyes; in another cage a long-winged kite was perched, the bird that in flight looks so much like an eagle; several venomous snakes lay about on the concrete floor of a pit.

A stocky man came around a cage and Sam spoke to him in German, asking him if he had strayed into a private zoo. The man made no reply, but could not take his eyes off the eagle. Feeling he had nothing to lose, Sam told him his story.

Desperate, he turned to the man. "Will you keep her for me until I can claim her?"

Time was running out.

The silent German, a fellow naturalist who knew the implications in taking the great bird—the caging and feeding difficulties—looked at Sam and nodded agreement.

Addresses were exchanged on scraps of paper, and Sam wrote down the essentials of feeding and care for his bird. He learned that his new friend's business, apart from his small collection of animals for his own interest and information, was milking snakes for the supply of antivenom serum needed by various institutes. Because of his authority and his use in this field, he was allowed ample land and any animals he wanted for study, and there was always a plentiful supply of animal foods.

The German rose and Sam followed him to look at a large aviary that had once held more than one bird of prey but now stood empty. There Sam left his dream bird, perched high on the lopped bough of a tree, and caught the train for his journey back to Wales, alone.

In the following year Sam received a postcard which was

a hand-painted eagle and the words *Weihnachten Grusse,* (Christmas Greetings). He knew this meant that his eagle was alive. Still later, an envelope arrived with an East German postmark. In it was a newspaper cutting in German that reported how a Berkut eagle was flown at a deer, and the deer was brought down during a recent competition. The forester dashed up to cut its throat and dragged the big eagle from its prey, which fellow falconers thought was a mistake, for he hooded the enormous bird without allowing her as much as a mouthful of her prey.

When a second deer was freed from the pen by the forester, he attempted to fly the eagle once again. The Berkut raked away from the deer and attacked the forester, taking him through the throat.

Then followed a few more lines on the condition of the forester and remarks on the impossibility of training a Berkut and the likelihood that she would never be allowed to fly in competition again. So the report ended.

Sam's distress at the consequences of handling his bird badly gave way to a feeling that there was more to this message he had received than just the story of an unfortunate incident in which his eagle was concerned. He thought that perhaps the Berkut's behavior might make her less welcome in the East.

Two years later, in 1960, a postcard giving the time of arrival of a plane in London sent him scurrying around making what arrangements he could for the Berkut's transshipment. He had too little notice to permit him time to get there himself, so he settled down in North Wales to wait for his lifelong dream to come true.

TWO

The complete falconer has an able body, a
quick spirit; to such a man a hawk will quickly
teach wisdom, but to him that wanteth wit she
will make a fool, and if a dull spirit, a trued
pack-horse.

—BERT'S APPROVED TREATISE 1619

A HATE-CRAZED bird en route to her owner crouched in
the belly of the last of a succession of planes that had
brought her from Eastern Europe to England's Heathrow
Airport.

The eagle inside the big wooden crate had nothing on
which her talons could grip, and she had suffered greatly
from the shifts and bounces of aircraft in flight during four
days of darkness, noise, hunger, and fear. By the time she
arrived at Heathrow she was in a towering rage.

The men who opened the crate had never seen such a
bird and were appalled when she catapulted out of the
crate uttering harsh screams of fury. Her pent up anger
over four days of cruel captivity was now turned on any liv-

ing thing in sight. At that time she weighed about twenty-four pounds, which in her natural state would enable her to take prey far larger than man. Her four-inch-plus talons could rip with bone-piercing power, and her nine-foot wings were capable of breaking a man's arm. Now they seemed to fill the hold of the plane with copper darkness.

The first casualty was an unfortunate cat. It was crushed instantly by the viselike talons and thrown aside, a limp, gray-furred bag. Frightened officials brought in an inspector from the RSPCA to get her back into her crate. He was fully aware of her terrible journey and wished only to provide her with food and water. But, sympathetic as he was, he was not an eagle-man and did not realize that what she needed right then was peace and reassurance rather than a few minutes' freedom and food. This miscalculation cost him a wounding from stabbing jabs of her talons.

Somehow the desperate wild thing was netted and wrongly given a barbiturate before being bundled into the crate in a stupefied condition. In the quiet that followed, amazed officials assessed the damage caused by this one predator to the plane itself. It totalled sixty-eight pounds!

Next, it was the turn of the customs, who were now responsible for the care of the eagle. According to regulations, a person must be at the airport to meet any animal consigned to him; he has to pay the costs plus a duty of twenty percent of its true value. Failure to comply requires the unlucky animal to be returned on the same plane. In the case of the Berkut this could not be done, as she had been transferred from one airline to another several times.

Sam had made what arrangements he could by telephone

for the eagle's arrival and found himself frantically trying to explain why she was so unique, repeating the story over and over to various officials to whom an eagle was merely a large bird with a hooked beak. He explained to a hotchpotch of customs' men that she was the only Berkut in the Western world and probably the largest known eagle; he repeated it to men at the London Zoo and to the unfortunate RSPCA man. To them the Berkut was officially an *Aquila Daphanea Hodgsoni,* the Eastern species of the golden eagle. They already knew the Scottish species, the *Aquila Chrysaetos,* but the Berkut was very much larger. He struck a chord when he reminded them that she was of the same family as Goldie, a famous eagle at the Regent's Park Zoological Gardens in London, but Goldie weighed about five pounds as against the Berkut's twenty-five. As value, size, and Latin names impress most human beings, Sam achieved a measure of success.

Another telephone call came for Sam, and then things began to move. The customs authorities, finding themselves with the largest eagle in the world on their hands and one made savage by her experiences, had no wish to keep her. An official telephoned Regent's Park Zoo to have a fair value put upon the bird, and then there was a final call to Sam.

Sam, frustrated by being so near to achieving his dream, agreed to pay transportation across London to Euston Station, then cash on delivery at Pwllheli, plus all the costs including making good the damage done to the plane during the eagle's short, frenzied battle for freedom.

Thus it was that on a July evening Sam stood on Pwllheli Station waiting for the Cambrian Coast express from Euston to bring his beautiful Berkut to him. He and a reporter friend, Ifan, watched the train clank and hiss to a stop, then hurried to the guard's van and together dragged the big crate onto the platform. The great bird was ominously silent as they loaded it onto the car.

Inside her prison, the tormented bird thrashed about as they drove along the bumpy roads of Pwllheli and on to the West End Parade where Sam lives in a big stone-fronted house. The Parade edges more than four miles of sandy beach along the shining sea, beyond which Tremadoc Bay is scooped out of the northern end of Cardigan Bay and the curving long arm of Lleyn Peninsula.

This is true eagle country, though its own magnificent heritage of free-flying golden eagles, plentiful during the eighteenth and nineteenth centuries, has long been wiped out by sportsmen, so that today only a few pairs remain in the remoter parts of Scotland.

To the north and east rise the hills of Wales, dominated by Mount Snowdon. Sam never looked at the craggy tips of these mountains, so much smaller than the Berkut's native Tien Shan range, without imagining great wings gliding over them in winter, the eagle in full yarak, the pale sun turning her plumage to gold.

The mountains in season are covered by many species of heather intermingling with butterwort and sundew and with saxifrages that bloom nowhere else except in the Arctic. In the wintertime the icy air, the sweep of sea and sky, the strong thermal current, and the world of craggy peaks are places over which to hunt and fly free.

The Welsh lyns (lakes) are fed by clear rivers of icy

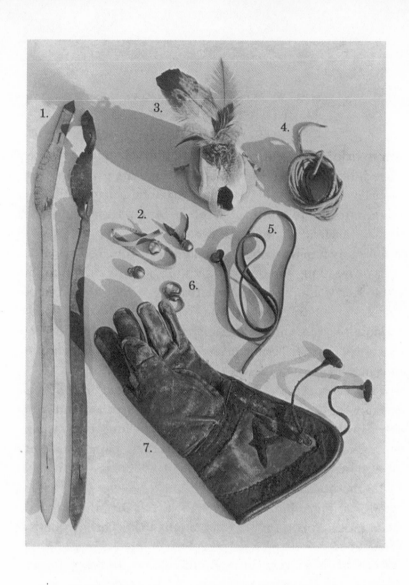

Atalanta had to be fitted immediately for training:
1. jesses, 2. bells, 3. hood, 4. nylon creance, 5. lease, 6. swivel, 7. gauntlet

mountain water tumbling down in cascading falls. The wide estuaries are backed by mountain ranges. The Lleyn Peninsula contains prehistoric burial chambers and hut circles, Iron Age and Roman forts, Welsh and English castles, and many a sturdy stone farmhouse marking man's occupation of the land since 2,000 B.C.

A still barbarous people enjoy the cruel pleasure of otter hunting and other so-called sports brought from the English plains by men driven into Wales by the early Saxon invaders. The oaths of these ancient people were sworn on their horns, falcons, hounds, and leashes; a man could not be summoned before a court after he had put on his boots in the morning; after that, he was beyond the reach of the law! Falconry was zealously pursued. The fourth office of the twenty-four high officers of the Welsh Court was that of the "great falconer," and he was allowed only three drafts of strong liquor lest he neglect his hawks. When he had a success with his falcon, the prince rose to greet him.

It was to this ancient land that the men drove the eagle. At the gate to Sam's home, he and Ifan removed the big wooden box. Inside the stuffy interior crouched the half-crazed Berkut. Sam, a man of outstanding courage and one of the finest falconers* in the world, knew that prolonged suffering made the eagle a potential danger to every living thing coming near her. Nevertheless, there was room in Sam's heart for nothing but elation.

Sam is a big man, over six feet tall, and extremely athletic, while his friend Ifan is smallish, with scanty blond

---

* In this case he would be called an austringer, the name given to those training short-winged hawks, among which the eagle is classified.

hair and pale blue eyes behind thick-lensed glasses. He is a keen newsman but lacks all knowledge of falconry and knows still less about eagles. Together they manhandled the crate through the door of Sam's home and up the stairs to his bedroom, which he had arranged to be in semidarkness. To a bird of prey, darkness suggests cover, safety, a time for sleep. But to the Berkut it suggested none of these things: not when she had suffered an exhausting journey from Eastern Europe, being bumped around in the imprisonment of the wooden box in the belly of a vibrating plane and harried during the frightening changes of plane. The darkness that reduced her sight to something more nearly approaching man's became, in the half-light, merely an additional fear.

Ifan was nervous but, fortunately for him, ignorant of the real danger. He saw only the shadowy blurs of the screen perch on which Sam hoped to perch his bird, the usual furniture, and the clumsy crate, a black square on the floor. But Sam knew that soon another blur would be added —a blur that was alive and full of menace, carrying the heavy armament of a four-inch beak, curved and molded through the ages by countless deaths, and steel-tipped daggers sharpened so that their strike could penetrate flesh and bone, for these are the birds that kill through crushing a skull or ribs or spine. To have this vast armory hidden in treacherous darkness was frightening.

Yet no man of Sam's courage and experience who waited for two years for this moment could allow fear to take it from him; above all, the eagle must not sense his flesh crawling away from her power to inflict pain.

With a minimum of bumping, the big box was put down on the floor of the bedroom. Sam straightened up, his heart thudding with excitement. The sheepskin jacket he wore as protection against the stabs of beak and talons and against the buffeting of those awesome wings was uncomfortly hot. Welder's armbands were pulled up to Sam's shoulders, and on his left hand he wore a gauntlet of buffalo hide which he had acquired in the East. The nervous tension built up in the next few seconds increased the feeling of suffocating heat. Now everything depended on him.

Ifan stood well away from the crate, and Sam reached back to the foot of the bed where he had thrown a black mackintosh. He handed this to Ifan.

"The eagle will come out of the crate like a rocket," he said. "It's your job to throw this over her so that I can get some control. If you foul it up, watch out for yourself! She could take your throat out or tear away half your face, and don't think she wouldn't! So be bloody careful."

Sam stood at the side of the crate. Slowly and quietly he lifted the sliding door out of its grooves and put it silently against the wall. The Berkut was free to leave her prison; the chances were she would come out of it a killer. There was no movement within the crate, nothing, just an uncanny stillness. Sam stooped to peer in at her. He whispered to his companion, "She's facing the wrong way! Give her tail a flick, that'll fetch her out."

"No damn fear, *you* do it!"

The twelve-feather span of her bedraggled tail was just inside the crate, while her fierce head faced the closed end. Sam tapped her tail. The crate exploded into a kind of clumsy dance. A heavy shape, with thrashing wings that seemed to fill the darkness, hurled itself across the room. Through the swishing and thudding of the air Sam's voice shouted: "Quick! Ifan! The mack—oh you bloody idiot!"

His shout was lost in the crashing of half-seen objects, "Watch the window. If she gets through the curtains she'll smash the glass and get away!"

No one heard this warning, because Ifan was already outside the door. He wanted no part of this shadowy demon that had gone berserk.

"Are you all right, Sam?" he shouted through the door.

Sam yelled back at him to go home, to come back tomorrow. All his concentration was needed for the job on hand. When a hunting bird is taken for training it must be fitted with jesses, two-foot-long strips of soft leather intricately slitted to fit comfortably around the legs; the swivel, two semicircles of metal joined by a pivoting rivet, holds the jesses over the top segment, while the bottom one takes the leash, eight feet of tough leather with a leather button at one end. With this, in the falconer's term, furniture the bird can be tied to a perch or handled on the fist.

Now Sam's first job was to get between the rampaging eagle and the window. With arms crossed to guard his face, he moved forward. A searing pain tore down his leg as the great talons raked him. The eagle fanned her tail and, using it for a springboard, sprang and embedded her talons in the sheepskin jacket. She tore at it with convulsive jerks. Lumps of the jacket came away as easily as if it had been made of cotton wool. Sam made a desperate grab with his gauntleted left hand at one of her feathered legs and groaned aloud as the panic-stricken eagle's talons pierced through the triple protection of leather sleeves, armband, and gauntlet.

The Berkut's harsh screams ripped through the air. The furious creature hung upside down from Sam's arm as he flopped her onto a table like a slaughtered turkey. The man was in an agonizing position when, luckily for him, she released her grip to perch upright. By now her struggles had somewhat sapped her energy. Even through his pain, Sam applauded her defiance. If he moved, the hackle feathers rose and she tensed for that fearful terrifying spring, the prelude to violent action.

Sam stood quietly, ignoring his own pain, talking incessantly, until he sensed that she had begun to accept his presence with lessened fear. The sound of his voice reassured her, possibly because through it she could pinpoint his position. Her dark bulk had a hypnotic stillness about it, and she allowed him to move closer to her. After a time she relaxed slightly and perched on one foot, drawing the other into the warmth of her feathered breast.

Sam possessed the infinite patience that is essential in falconry. For more than an hour he stood whispering to his bird. Then he moved stealthily to reach the rabbit's hindquarters that he had prepared for this moment. He held it before her. In an instant she was balanced on both feet, tense as boxer on guard, her wings curved outward from hunched, muscular shoulders, ready to attack.

For half an hour the man forced his weary arm to remain steady. Gradually the bird's tenseness receded. She eyed the piece of rabbit through the semidarkness. Suddenly, a mighty talon flashed out and tore the haunch from his hand. As she took stand on her prey, she looked shapeless and enormous in the half-light. She drove her talons into the haunch, mantling it with spread wings and tail to protect it from intruders.

This was a natural instinct, and Sam was glad it had survived her long ordeal. She tore at the rabbit, gulping fur, bones, and flesh, and as she ate she chattered a warning to him to keep his distance. It would be a foolish man who would attempt to take an eagle's prey under those conditions!

Sam was acutely aware of his unprotected face as he stood before the wild creature knowing the time had come for action. His fair hair dampened with sweat and a cold sweat broke out over his body. The next move must be his, and it was possible to make it only while she was absorbed in her food. That was his one chance of fitting the jesses, and until that was done he had no control at all over her. Moreover, before he could tether her he must also fit her hood, and it was important not to frighten her or to allow her to throw herself about or to bate. Bating is the frantic beating of a bird's wings as it throws itself backward in a crazy protest against captivity, and it could damage feathers that would take a year or more to grow back after a moult.

As quietly as possible Sam went to work. The least jerky movement could upset the bird crouching before him. The thought of that curved scimitar of a beak tearing at his flesh made him shudder. The eagle was ravenous, hunger blotted out her instinct to strike at him. Raking talons can inflict dreadful injury to a man's eyes and face, and as the gnome-like creature was perched on a level with Sam's shoulders the danger was considerable. But there was nothing he could do about it.

Sam has trained many birds of prey—some to hunt, others as pets; but this enormous bird before him was a falconer's dream and not subject to the laws that govern lesser birds. She was a Berkut, the eagle of the Tartar emperors, and no bird possesses as vile a temper. All Berkuts are said to be untamable because of this hair-trigger touchiness, and this one had been unmanned for so long that she retained nothing of her former training, she was as completely wild as any bird among the crags. Sam's approach was to a savage and resentful killer. What the Eastern berkutschi wants from the finished product and the methods he uses are very different from the Western falconer's ideas of training. This bird would never again endure the cruel seeling of the eyelids that render the chained hunters less dangerous. The few lessons suited to such primitive mastery were far less complex in pattern than the obedience through love that Sam wanted from his bird.

Sam was proud of his ability to fit jesses; he had been known to do it one-handed in seven seconds flat. But he doubted if it was possible to fit them at all onto an angry eagle of the Berkut's size. Sure enough, two hours after he attempted to secure her, she was still minus her jesses.

It was 10 P.M. before darkness really fell and midnight before the jesses were fitted onto the eagle's heavily feathered legs. Sam tugged at the chewed-over rabbit haunch and she began to scream the nerve-jangling cry of the furious eagle. Her screams changed to an angry chattering and she dug her talons convulsively into the mangled rabbit, mantling it closely. So Sam accomplished his mission by stealth. She was so intent on holding her prey that she did

A butcher's block weighted by barbells stood ready to receive Atalanta

not resist when Sam threaded the leather thongs around legs with a circumference of six and a quarter inches.

When the jesses were secured, Sam knew that he had won the first round. He still had to fit the swivel and the leash to the long jesses, but he could do that expertly even in the darkness. When it was done he sighed with relief; now his beautiful eagle was more nearly manageable.

It took a few minutes to get her into the right position to slip the plumed, goatskin hood over her head. With a quick movement he pulled the thongs at the back of the hood into place so that it fitted exactly. The eagle was furnished.

He put his gauntleted hand under her clutching foot and raised his fist as the hooded bird stepped onto it. Sam's pride was immense as the weary eagle perched proudly on his fist, putting her great weight on his arm. Her reflexes anticipated his movements as a dancer follows her partner. She balanced as though she were on the branch of a windswept tree; in his heart he felt great tenderness for this proud creature he must tame.

Sam gathered up the jesses and the leash and tied her firmly to his fist, not really believing his luck. The mighty talons closed on the gauntlet to help her retain her balance, and the power in them brought tears of pain into his eyes. This was cheerfully borne as he carried her downstairs. On his fist was not just an eagle of a never-before-known size, it was a dream come true. He owned and would train the greatest hunting bird in the world; she would learn to fly free, to hunt her own food, and to return to his fist on command.

Killer talons span 11½ inches from front to back.
Back talon alone is 4¼ inches
© B. R. Tullis

THREE

All the flowers of tomorrow are in the seeds of today.
—CHINESE PROVERB

SAM carried the hooded bird onto the lawn in front of the house, where a butcher's block stood ready to receive her. He tethered her to a bar bell weighing one hundred and fifty-six pounds, a necessary safeguard. He knew that the moment he slipped her hood she would go berserk in her strange surroundings.

It had been an exhausting struggle. Seeing a light in the kitchen, Sam went indoors and ordered tea and sandwiches to be brought out to him on the lawn. He returned and propped himself against the wall, munching hungrily.

Very slowly some of the exhaustion ebbed from his body. After the long ordeal in the darkened room, the warm night and the salty air brought him the respite he needed

Sam lived in his sheepskin jacket until Atalanta settled down

© *B. R. Tullis*

for the battle he knew must come. He sat there in his necessarily thick clothing, his body saturated with sweat and aching from weariness. He could not look away from his bird as he tried to assess her physical injuries; only time would disclose the emotional ones.

Sam felt the muscular tension lessen, but the weariness remained. He leaned back against the wall and gathered strength into his tired body, knowing he had taken the first step on the long road that lay before him. He fought to relax, closing his eyes to shut out the eagle that filled his world. Yesterday when he and Ifan had hauled the crate onto the Pwllheli platform, he had noted she had blood on her head and was trailing one wing. Since then he had had no opportunity to see what damage had been done to the freed bird in the darkened room.

Sam opened his eyes. It was the night of July 14, and the frenzied holiday season was in full swing. Like a weary commander, Sam took a last look around before plunging back into battle. It was not a peaceful scene. While there were no "blacksmiths' forges nor glittering fires" to which, as Gervaise Markham said in 1615, all hawks should become accustomed, the Parade before the lawn on which the eagle waited was ablaze with lights. Floodlights from the hotel next door threw rays of unnatural colors across the lawn and onto the block on which the hooded eagle stood. Even the grass gleamed with false colors. Traffic roared by, sports car owners gunned their motors, drowning out the shouts of drunken men. These were bad surroundings in which to unhood a mountain-bred Berkut. But it was also the world in which she must live and be sure of Sam's protection, and the sooner she accepted this the better it would be for both of them.

As an expert falconer, Sam had no illusions about the difficulties facing him before his Berkut could be trained. He had only to recall the experiences of the late Captain Charles Knight, who attempted to fly his Scottish golden eagle Grampion. As he recounted it in his book *The Golden Eagle,* published in 1927, although he protected himself by wearing a fencing mask, the bird buried an inside talon in his cheek and the hind talon through his ear; he was lucky not to lose an eye. Two more such unfortunate accidents decided Captain Knight not to fly female golden eagles again because of their aggressive and uncertain tempers.

Much the same reaction came from the British Falconers Club. Of the two hundred and twenty-five members who belonged to the club, only twenty-three flew hawks at game in Great Britain; six hunted with long-winged hawks. And the club recommended that the members leave golden eagles alone because their fierceness and temper make them useless for falconry. Sam decided to prove that the golden eagle was the best hawk of all!

Sam unhooded his eagle with a neatness born of practice and steeled himself for what he knew must happen. With the darkness, the night became filled with menace: the roaring cars, the shouting men, and the artificial brightness of colored lights—all were too much for the highly strung bird; she began to bate.

The bating of a hawk is a terrible thing to see, rather as if a child was filled with temporary madness. Bating is a wild eagle's reaction to captivity. She throws herself backward off fist or perch in an insane repetition, beating her wings, thrusting out her tongue, hissing and fluttering wildly, moving her powerful wings with a crazy nervous intensity. Had she been short-tied but able to reach the end of the leash, the terror-ridden creature would have smashed her great wings by crashing them repeatedly into the ground. The size of the Berkut made all this even more frightening because Sam feared that he might not be able to prevent her doing herself some permanent harm.

Fortunately she was still tied to the bar bell. Whenever the bating lessened, a car would roar by or a group of noisy people would pass and trigger off this nervous reaction—an instinctive effort to escape at whatever cost. She fluttered wildly across the lawn and her massive wingbeats and sturdy legs dragged the hundred and fifty-six pound bar bell after her.

As an exhibition of winged strength, this fear-engendered feat will probably never be equalled; in those days she was a young bird and lighter than she is today. Her spread-winged progression was awkward looking, as are most eagles' movements on the ground, but it kept her wings from serious injury. Before she became exhausted, she dragged the bar bell, which was nearly eight times her own weight, the whole length of the lawn.

Sam watched her unhappily, realizing that he had underestimated her strength. His difficulty was how to get her safely back onto her block after each bate. When he went near the gasping bird, her hackle feathers rose and she hissed her warning and raked at him with her steel-hooked talons. For a time the problem seemed insoluble. To get her onto Sam's fist meant real danger, even though the gauntlet reached to the elbow, but there was no way of putting her onto the block without carrying.

Nevertheless, whenever he tried to get the distressed creature onto his arm, it turned into a painful fiasco. In spite of her screaming and bating, her fierce strikes, and her fear, Sam felt that much of her violence was a kind of desperate bluff and that when this phase passed and nothing dire happened to her, she would settle down and acknowledge that he was her friend.

Part of the trouble was that, like most wild things, she could smell fear, and he knew that he was very afraid and in a way he had never experienced before. Forcing himself to show confidence that deep down he did not really feel and averting his face, he managed to pull one enormous taloned foot onto his gauntlet. The Berkut was nearly exhausted and did not rake her talons at his face. Instead she did something unpredictable: clamping her talons on his arm with her foot almost enveloping the gauntlet, her powerful foot contracted through the buffalo-skin gauntlet, the welder's armband, the leather sleeve of the sheepskin jacket, and deep into the flesh and sinew of his arm. The viselike grip of the eagle when back and front talons meet in one tremendous squeeze drove the talons inward until they penetrated the elbow joint. The pain was dizzying.

Sam waited grimly for it to subside enough for him to go on with the training. Someone phoned for a doctor. Tired and wracked with pain, Sam forced himself to concentrate on his eagle. Not only is the elbow sensitive, but the gauntlet had formerly been baited with food and the danger of infection was great. The doctor arrived, unasked for by Sam, who angrily refused treatment. Luckily, the doctor had met Sam earlier, thought him a little mad, and was able to persuade him that he must have an antitetanus injection.

By now it was plain to see that the bedraggled but still dangerous bird could not be trained as hawks and falcons are, by hunger. Hunger pains in this giant thing only brought on a continual, spasmodic gripping of talons, and anything that moved seemed to her potential food— including her trainer—an obsession that could bring disaster. Sam smiled grimly to himself, remembering how "stout Cortez," in the days of the conquistadores, lost his forefinger to a South American harpy eagle.

In her way, the Berkut was teaching Sam by making it clear what she would and would *not* do, while he clung grimly to the fact that before he could train her he had to tame her, man her with a thoroughness that would prevent tragedy. A man and his hawk are indivisible. To train an eagle, a falconer must always follow its instincts; it is not for him to create a regime in opposition to his hawk's disposition at the time. All training schedules must follow the cycle of the seasons. A hawk is an ever-changing creature in character and in the physical expression that accompanies each cycle. Man must follow this pattern, he cannot force his own desire upon it. The trainer must have an awareness of the bird's instincts and anticipate and then use the changes as they occur.

For the bird, and for its trainer if he knows what he is doing, there will be the season of the hunter, a time when the disciplined killer is in full yarak (zest) ; the moult, when the bird may be grumpy and as touchy as any invalid needing intelligent nursing; a time of loving gentleness and gaiety when the hawk turns dilettante and is amused and amusing; a time of tenderness, when the great bird sickens of love, and prepares for her eggs which mark the half-birth of her nestlings; and then the ineffable peace and happiness that brooding her young brings to her. The wise, successful, and devoted trainer builds on the solid foundations of these passing phases. Sam is a master at anticipating instinct, which is one of the things that make him a truly great trainer.

Now Sam tried to forget his pain as he made a decision. Her training must be done in three phases. First, he must gain her confidence, and that alone would be difficult enough with a bird of her size, ferocity, and uncertain temper. In the second stage he would feed her well, so well that she would become placid and sluggish. Third, and dominating all three stages, confidence must become affection between them, and that would take infinite skill and patience, because a hunting bird must never become a pet bird.

These thoughts churned through his mind as he fought to keep his mind off the pain in his arm. Somehow he must get the unhappy, breathless eagle back onto her block. There was too much movement all around, too many noises for him to take her up again onto his fist to carry her back, so there was only one way: he must make use of that noise and movement to drive her back onto her block.

Like so many birds which are magical in flight, an eagle

is a clumsy thing on the ground, and this one moved pon-
derously as she continued to bate, dragging the bar bell in
response to every new disturbance. But even her fear and
anger could not quite swamp her intelligence. She learned
that all the tremendous effort she was making brought her
no joy, and that the only place of peace for her was on the
butcher's block. When she realized this, Sam was able to
shoo the struggling, wing-bashing bird back onto her perch.

Sam prepared himself for the first nightlong vigil. He
knew that part of the bird's explosive strength had been
spent. The safest way to exhaust the eagle would be not to
sap her powers or force her to make efforts that were beyond even her great strength, these could cause her physical and nervous damage. Exhaustion could be achieved by
keeping her awake, an age-old weapon in the falconers'
armory.

So this is what Sam decided to do, and if necessary he
would keep at it for a week. The tired but unbroken creature must not be allowed to sleep until she allowed him to
touch her lanceolate headfeathers without protest; then she
could sleep. "And so, by God, will I!" Sam muttered to
himself.

Already the Berkut recognized his voice. She carried
within her all the quick suspicions of a wild thing, and during her early training it was important for the man to look
always exactly the same to her. This meant that Sam must
live in his sheepskin jacket, which was already ripped and
torn by her talons, a white, roll-neck sweater, and the same
trousers and shoes. Like all short-winged hawks, eagles can
see colors and they are very sensitive to the slightest change

in their trainer's appearance; a scarf of unaccustomed color would be enough to start her bating.

All night long Sam battled with his fierce charge. At dawn the personal battle between man and eagle still went on. Sam's eyes were heavy with sleep, but he dared not give in. Man and bird fought more fiercely as the sun mounted and became warm and golden in the clear sky. Eagles, because of their high body temperature, approximately $111°$ F, cannot stand direct sunshine for long. As the heat intensified, the eagle increased her efforts to find a way out of it.

The movement of the traffic became louder. Tradesmen called. It was still early when a crowd of people collected outside the low wall that divided the lawn from the Parade. They watched the furiously bating eagle dragging the heavy bar bell across the lawn, sometimes collapsing with her great wings spread. Sam was filled with a guilty sadness that he must drive this splendid wild creature beyond the limit of its endurance for his own ends. She seemed to possess almost incredible reserves of strength.

Time went on. Sam was all in. With every alien movement of a car or the crowd, a new problem presented itself. By 10 A.M. the sweating, exhausted falconer decided to leave a boy with a stirrup pump and orders to spray the panting feathered menace, while her trainer went indoors to have breakfast. This, as things turned out, was an almost fatal mistake.

Sam went into the house leaving the wet, bedraggled chrysanthemum of an eagle lying with outspread wings on the grass, eyeing him balefully and giving an occasional harsh, indignant croak.

As Sam disappeared, Ifan reappeared carrying his camera. He felt rather important as he pushed his way through the crowd of sightseers. Daniel approaching the lions, he bravely slipped the catch on the gate and advanced boldy in the general direction of the eagle. Disregarding shouts from the bathers and the shifting population along the wall, he advanced to within twenty feet of the eagle, which watched his approach with a kind of ferocious intensity. For Ifan this was the signal to keep what he called "a safe distance."

Camera in hand, the young man concentrated on his task. The eagle's hackle feathers rose, but the warning signal meant nothing to Ifan.

Any uncertain-tempered, nervous bird probably would have been irritated by the man and his clicking camera. Now Ifan was almost finished; he wanted only one more photograph: an impressive shot of her massive wings at full stretch. But he did not know how to make her lift and spread them.

To Ifan's mind, opening its wings should present no problem to a bird, even one as large as this; probably all she needed was some prodding. So, with camera swinging, he jumped up and down in a side-straddle hop. The spectators' voices sank to a whisper as they watched the grotesque performance . . . arms at side . . . legs apart . . . arms flung upward. . . .

The eagle seemed as astonished as the spectators. She cocked her head and kept her frowning eyes on the display. Ifan began to puff.

"Open up! Open up! Damn you!" he panted.

Almost as if the eagle replied "Certainly!" the Berkut opened her wings and hit Ifan head on at waist height. "Like a great plank coming through the air at me," he described it later. Her out-thrust talons pierced his jacket and catapulted him backward, his camera shot up in the air, flew over the hedge, and crash-landed on the hard pavement. Poor Ifan was driven backward over the front gate, bating almost like an eagle himself, buttons torn from his jacket and a piece of cloth ripped out. The Berkut squatted back and tore at it savagely while she kek-kek-kekked her rage.

Sam, bone weary and unconscious of all the drama, had just sat down thankfully to begin breakfast when he heard the disturbance from the lawn. He rushed out, followed by his mother, a tiny indomitable lady of over eighty.

Sam saw what had happened and, shouting unprintable names at Ifan, went to do what he could for the Berkut. Sam's mother helped the shattered newsman through the door and Sam soon had things under control.

After the diversion caused by Ifan, the hard slogging of manning began. Three nights went by without sleep, until both Sam and his eagle were deathly weary.

It was July, a time of alternating sunshine and showers, and the sleepless nights became almost unbearable. Sam seized upon the opportunity to do anything he could for his stubborn bird. He constantly sprayed her plumage. The damage done to her in the crate lessened, her wing no longer drooped, the gash on her proud head became bare and clean. As she lost much of her pitifully bedraggled appearance, she began to gain some aura of her own special power and glory. She roused and preened herself in sunshine that turned her to shining copper.

The average golden eagle female of the British species weighs around twelve pounds, with a seven-foot wingspan. Even at that time the Berkut's weight almost doubled the average and her wingspan was an awesome nine feet.

Most of the time, the eagle sat quietly enough on her block. But the instant Sam stretched out a friendly hand she began her warning "kek-kek-kek!" and clenched and unclenched her talons menacingly.

In time, Sam sensed that his eagle had his measure quite as accurately as he had hers. At times it seemed they had reached stalemate, and sometimes Sam felt almost unbearably tired and discouraged. He told himself that he should be satisfied with the progress he and his eagle had made together, but the uneasiness persisted. After training many hawks and falcons, Sam believed he understood his eagle's uncooperativeness. None of her moods were new to him. She was obstinate and flash-tempered, but still there was something else he could not understand about her, and it worried him.

After the evening of her arrival she had refused all food, which was not entirely surprising.

For three nights he had kept the bird, and himself, without sleep. It was the fifth evening and so far she had refused all food and did not seem to want to sleep. Strangely, she appeared to be as powerful as ever, in contrast to her master who yearned for a few hours of trouble-free sleep and for even the smallest success with her manning.

That Sunday evening she suddenly began to eat. Her austere, death-dealing head shook from side to side and she vomited from deep within the pannel of her stomach. It was a wrenching effort for her. Then, from her beak fell a soft, green lump. Sam stared at it with puzzled eyes. It could have been a lump of plasticine by its color and texture, the sort of thing that children use for modeling.

As Sam held the strange casting in his hand, he became aware he was not alone. A spectator leaned over the wall and, in a voice with a Scottish accent, asked Sam if he could examine the casting. He explained he was a doctor.

Sam gratefully handed the casting to the doctor, who examined it carefully and came up with the opinion that it was a barbiturate that by all known rules should have poisoned her. Sam, remembering the airport incident, realized that only the peculiarities of the eagle's digestive system had saved his bird's life. Luckily she had not digested the barbiturate in her stomach, but retained it in the pannel from which she was evidently able to bring it up undigested as a casting.

All eagles need regular supplies of fur, feathers, and bones. These are known as roughage or castings and without them the eagle dies. The purpose of these castings is to revolve slowly around the small pannel (the bird's abdominal intestines), collecting mucous and indigestible foods such as gristle. This internal churning binds the residue into a compact oval for regurgitation as a casting or pellet.

About an hour after she had cast the barbiturate, Sam noticed a change in his eagle. While still uneasy and appre-

For Sam these were days of "battle and torture"
© *S. Barnes*

The big Berkut in Sam's front yard; it was a miracle.

hensive if he moved near to her, he had the feeling that his patience was creating a tenuous bond of trust between them. Now that the poisonous casting was out of her system she probably felt better, she might even become conscious of the fact that it was Sam who had shared her captivity for the past five long days and nights; he alone had cared for her, braved the treacherous weather, endured the people, the lights, the noise, and he too had gone without sleep.

Whatever caused the subtle change in her attitude, it was generous reward for Sam's long-drawn patience with this rare, savage, and hitherto untamable creature.

He had never known a challenge and excitement so great. Sam knew that there can be no shortcuts in training a bird of prey, and he did not allow himself any slackness. But at last there was some sign of response.

Sam went off and returned with half a rabbit. He stood by the block on which the Berkut perched, knowing that she must be tired and hungry. He also knew her indomitable will. He was in for a surprise. The ponderous bird moved like a flash and pounced on the piece of rabbit as if it had been live prey. Then she screamed, working herself into a rage in defense of her prey, and in her anger at the mere thought of a marauder daring to challenge her, she drove her talons into the limp body again and again. Then she took stand on the tattered thing and began to gorge, tearing at it, swallowing lumps of flesh and fur and bones.

The sight of the ravenous creature delighted Sam. He laughed with pleasure and began playing with her, drawing her closer to him while she clung tenaciously to the torn piece of rabbit. The excited eagle ate as quickly as possible, and she did not strike at Sam.

It was later the same evening, his tall body sagging with weariness as he forced the fog of sleep from his brain, that Sam had his first great triumph. Comfortably gorged, the eagle perched herself on one leg and drew the other doubled-up fist into the warmth of her breast feathers. She allowed him to feel her crop; it was packed as round as a cricket ball with rabbit.

Then Sam achieved what was for him a supreme delight, for she allowed him to tickle her marvelous, sculptured head as she closed her eyes from sheer exhaustion and dozed contentedly—but only for as long as his gently moving fingers stayed on her head.

The tired man stood on his lawn with the eagle's fierce, streamlined head beneath his moving fingers. Already in his sleep-touched imagination were visions of the Berkut in free flight over the rugged mountains of Snowdonia. It was a dream such as Kublai Khan, emperor of the Mongols, knew in Xanadu, for Kublai Khan was one of the great hawk masters of old and he hunted with ten thousand falconers carrying eagles, great Berkuts, in the splendid days when falconry was born in the East. Only emperors flew Berkuts; the lords carried falcons proud on their fists, and the lesser of the noble hawks, the toscaols, or hawk watchers, went with them. Around every hawk's leg was a silver ring with its owner's name engraved on it. The Khan's love of the chase was so tyrannical that neither tradesman nor husbandman was allowed to keep any bird for the pursuit of game. Sam hoped he would be luckier than Coleridge with his dreams of Xanadu broken by the "person from Porlock." Sam's dream was still intact, all twenty-odd pounds of it.

For the first time in five days it seemed to Sam that the fragile bond he believed forming between his hawk and himself might prove to be something more than fancy.

FOUR

*The essence of falconry is not in the flight or
the kill, but man's relation with his hawk.*
—T. H. WHITE

ONCE the poisonous barbiturate was out of her system, the
Berkut began to mellow a bit toward her training. Sam was
pleased to see that her hair-trigger temper was not ruined,
as it might well have been. Daily he realized that she possessed the invaluable combination of pride and humility
without which no bird of prey can accept discipline. If she
accepted him as master, she must respect him; but this was
not yet the time for that decisive battle of wills, the battle
Sam knew he must win or forever lose his dream.

As the days passed there was no more than a suggestion of
give and take between them. The strength of her wings, the
lethal strike of her talons remained facts to be conjured
with. She still bated furiously, she was disdainful of every-

thing human. One move from her trainer and she would raise her hackle feathers belligerently. She fought against any lowering of the barriers of distrust she had raised between them.

Then one day Sam felt her rugged ferocity was lessening and realized that the final battle must come soon. Pressing a momentary advantage, he tried to get her onto his fist. This was humiliating for the royal bird. Each attempt ended in failure, not only because of her resistance but because the movement was difficult with her short-tied to the heavily weighted bar bell.

It was a hot, sultry afternoon. Sam sweated and panted from the exertion of trying to untie her. He substituted a nylon creance with a two-thousand-pound breaking strain, long enough to give her the freedom of the whole lawn.

This done, Sam baited his gauntlet with a chickenhead, hoping she would fly to his fist for it. The eagle became sullen and ignored the bait. Sticky with heat and exhausted by his day and night attendance on her, he suddenly felt desperate and flung the chicken head down on the butcher's block. The eagle pounced on it instantly and began to tear at it. This was the moment. Sam moved behind the unsuspecting bird and tore the chicken head from her bloodied talons.

Every nerve in the great body quivered with fury, her feathers shook in outrage. He had violated her rights. For this affront to her pride she would, in her wild state, have attacked her mate, even her young. Under the law of her mountain heritage her simple answer to insult was "Attack!"

The Berkut, poised shoulder high to Sam, launched herself at him, kek-kekking her rage. Her outspread wings filled the air with darkness and she swept forward, legs extended, determined to tear down the despoiler of her prey.

Sam knew when he was beaten. He simply turned his back, ducked his head, and ran, hoping to get beyond the length of the creance before the fury reached him. He was too late. With the terrifyingly harsh scream of the angry eagle she hit him, embedding her talons in his sheepskin-clad shoulders with such force that he stumbled forward out of balance and fell on his knees. Fortunately the eagle overshot the length of the creance.

This saved Sam momentarily. The creance dragged the eagle to the ground, her talons clutching the torn out lump of jacket, and the man and his eagle squatted on the earth, their heads level. This was what Sam wanted. The Berkut was out of her element, heavy and cumbersome in her movements on the ground, cut down to a man's size.

Sam jumped back into the arena of the lawn. The time had come to settle, once and for always, who was going to be master, and he meant it to be himself. On the strip of lawn around the butcher's block, the eagle and her trainer fought out their duel. At first neither gained the advantage. Sam allowed the Berkut to do all the attacking. He parried her fierce thrusts by using the thick jacket as a matador uses the cape; he feinted and moved his feet continuously like a boxer. He thrust his dummy enemy at the clumsy eagle so that at the end of each feint he finished up either sideways or behind the attacking Berkut.

The eagle made each of her attacks the same way. She

waddled across the lawn with her copper feathers quivering and trailed her wings in a manner as menacing as the hunched shoulders of a thug. Then she crouched, her head low and moving from side to side with the sinister ferocity of a python measuring its prey. Using her splayed tail as a springboard, she thrust at him with extended legs and flashing talons, which she brought down in fast and deadly convulsive blows.

Sam kept close to the furious bird but always just out of her reach. He dared not make the fatal mistake of allowing her enough room to launch herself through the air at him. Always he had to remember that under no circumstance must he hurt her physically. If he did that, and it would be easy to do accidentally, he would lose forever the chance to gain his eagle's love and trust. No bird of prey would ever forget such an experience.

The Berkut was fighting mad, she battled on until she was at the point of exhaustion, panting like a winded animal. Now it was easier for Sam to dodge what had become waddling, clumsy attacks. He decided to change his tactics. The eagle attacked and he parried; he jumped behind her and stood on the creance, pressing it into the grass close behind her jess-fitted legs. This made her helpless and held her on the ground. He stooped quickly and, before she had time to realize what was happening, he gripped each sturdy leg just above the talons and hoisted her into the air. In this position she was defenseless and could not resist him as he carried her about the lawn. The great wolf-killing Berkut was beaten, and she knew it!

The question still remained, which of them was going to

be absolute master? When the time came for him to release his grip on her legs, the eagle was neither panicky nor frightened. She could have struck at him with her potentially lethal beak, but she did not. It had been a fair contest; the loss of some of her regal bearing no longer mattered. She was exhausted, she knew she must resign herself to Sam and admit defeat.

Half an hour later, an overjoyed Sam put her down on her butcher's block without any difficulty and without ruffling a single sleek feather not already damaged by her brutal journey.

Sam went indoors, put up a screen perch in his bedroom, came down again, and brought the Berkut indoors and short-tied her to her perch. This was progress. But capitulation to her master did not rob the Berkut of all of her wild aggressiveness. She recovered her strength and toppled herself and her perch several times onto the floor. Sam soon had to reinforce the legs of the perch so that it would hold her fiercely bating body. He made it secure enough to withstand her most violent onslaughts.

Within two hours of beginning her heavy bating, she climbed back onto the screen perch without help. Sam was greatly pleased, for many birds of prey do not learn to do this and hang upside down until they die. Usually a falconer teaches his hawks to reclaim themselves, and it is a test of patience. A hunting bird that bates off the fist should never be helped back again; it must learn to pull itself back by leash and jesses. The same technique applies to the screen perch where, if she does not learn for herself, she might die if her trainer is absent.

Finally the big Berkut decided to accept the perch as she had accepted the man, and she slept contentedly. Sam's nervously alert mind refused sleep. The Berkut was here, in his own home; it was a miracle, one he could not bear let slip from his consciousness.

He lay quietly in the dark room, his eyes on the bay window, as the outside light turned the silhouette of his bird into a wedge of solid blackness. She perched there, a triangle decapitated by the darkness, her splendid head buried between her shoulders in the miraculous manner of eagles never fathomed by man. The darkness blotted out the copper gleam of her feathers, making it appear she had no head at all; she snuggled into the warmth of her heavily feathered shoulders, where the eagles who live on high have their alula, or bastard wings—which are especially fine in Berkuts—covering them like the feathered capes of Aztec kings, providing warmth and helping to stabilize their flight.

Dawn lightened the sky, but her master lay awake, still unable to believe his great luck.

FIVE

*The sons of noblemen should wind their
horn, carry fair their hawks, and leave study
and learning to the meaner people.*
—ADVICE TO A YOUTH IN THE TIME OF KING JAMES I

ACCORDING to one legend, falconry began in the land
once called Scythia, which is now the Ukraine. Other legends place its origin in Korea and China. On at least one
point, however, all the legends agree: throughout the ages,
falconry has been the most delicately emotional, fiercely
beautiful, and elemental pursuit of game. Two thousand
years before Christ, European kings hawked, their falcons
waited-on, circling above their masters' heads, or were
thrown from their fists to slice the sky with their pointed
wings and take their prey in two-hundred-mile-an-hour
stoops, while the wind thundered through their pinions.
History and legend alike have been interwoven with the
proud and deadly bird the falconer holds on his fist.

Eagle legends are varied in origin and interpretation.

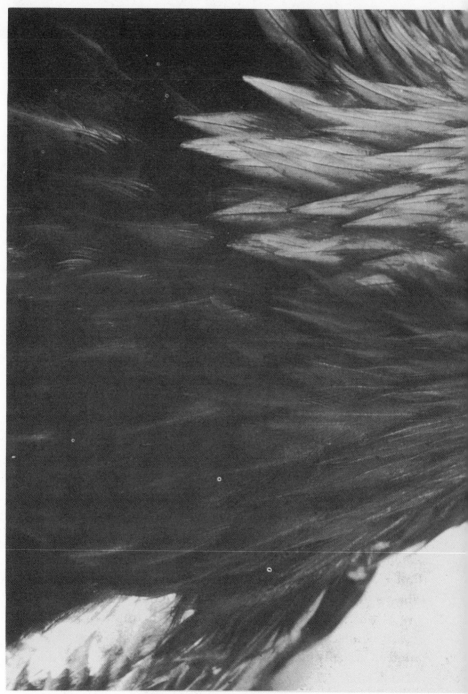
Royal eagle of the Tartars, hunter of Genghis Khan, Kublai Khan, the czars

Poets have sung of them; they are the symbols of national pride, of luck, and of eternal youth. They have been credited with the possession and exercise of supernatural powers. Hawks have been the adornment of the crimson and gold courts of the past.

In the first century Pliny was said to be the first man to write of falconry in Europe. He had strange fancies connecting eagles with stones. According to him, the stones found near an eagle's nest gave the man who took them the power to make himself invisible. Eagles are the only birds that cannot be killed by lightning, said Pliny, who also believed them to possess the coveted power of rejuvenation. Firstly the eagle must find a well, then it must fly above it, so close to the sun that its feathers are scorched. When it dives into the well, the feathers will become perfect and its vision clear.

Hence, to the Romans the eagle was of great symbolic importance. It was a bird of good omen and was chosen to carry the souls of departed warriors from the funeral pyre to immortality. The bird was also the emblem of the conquering Roman legions. Originally, it was an uncle of Julius Caesar who presented the Roman Army with its first silver and gold eagles for their standards on triumphal occasions. The eagle, bird of their god Jove, was a fitting emblem for the victorious legions. Their standards were surmounted by eagles carrying the thunderbolts of Jove clasped in their talons. It was a dire disgrace to lose an eagle standard in battle.

For other, less aggressive civilizations of the time, the eagle signified more pacific virtues. Witness the account in

Exodus of the Lord's call to Moses in the desert of Sinai, "I bare you on eagle's wings, and brought you unto Myself." The Greeks also valued the eagle's protection and burned the right wing of an eagle in their vineyards to guard against hailstones. Old writers claimed that certain of the eagle's bodily organs had a medicinal value—marrow, for instance. Even as late as the Middle Ages, people were not aware that the bones of birds of prey contain no marrow.

Even earlier than this, a legend behind a legend of an Iranian king named Sam concerned itself with the protective image of the eagle. The son of this king was born with white hair, much to the embarrassment of his father. Sam's advisers told him his child was a demon, and so the baby was abandoned near the nest of the great Simurgh, a gigantic eagle like the Roc of Sinbad's time.

The Simurgh took the child, but instead of devouring him she brought him up. Sam dreamed that his son was alive and searched for him. The Simurgh took the boy in her great talons and bore him to his father. She made a tender speech of farewell to the child, whose name was Zal, and Zal wept. The Simurgh plucked a feather from her breast saying, "In your day of need cast this feather upon the fire, and I will come to you."

Years later when Zal's wife lay dying in childbirth, Zal summoned the Simurgh. So the hero, Rustum, was born by Caesarean birth, attended by the Simurgh.

The eagle was probably first used as a device for banners by the Assyrians; Attila the Hun was tough enough to take his ease in a stone armchair, as any visitor to Torcello can testify, but he verged on the sentimental over his goshawks, using them as his own device on three separate articles of apparel.

Germany's eagle was originally single-headed; it was adopted by Charlemagne as the symbol of empire after his coronation in Rome in A.D. 800. Then in 802, when he wished to unite Rome and Germany, he added the second head. Ludwig of Bavaria had eagle-stamped coins struck in the fourteenth century. The eagle continued to dominate the arms of the Holy Roman Empire until its destruction.

Poland filched its white eagle on a red ground from a legend symbolizing fidelity. When the country became Christian under King Mieczyslaw in the tenth century, so the story goes, a wood was cut down to make room for the celebration, destroying the nest of a white eagle and causing the young to fall to the ground. The mother refused to abandon them and she died there with her young.

Some say the Romans brought falconry to Britain; certainly in the seventh century Ethelbert, a Saxon monarch, sent to Germany for a cast of falcons to fly at cranes. Alfred the Great, derided as a cook, was such a proficient falconer that he wrote a treatise on hawking.

The great influence of falconry through more than nine hundred years of England's history is often forgotten by historians. Falconry flourished from about the eighth century until the advent of the sporting rifle and the fencing of farmlands in the mid-seventeenth century. Guns can be put away; hawks cannot. When fashionable society began to spend the winter season in towns such as London, Bath, and

Tunbridge Wells, it became difficult to maintain hawks in a fit condition.

The Saxon kings were all keen falconers. They added the mighty gyrfalcons, captured from Viking foes, to mews that had housed only peregrines. These gyrs were a bonus from the Norsemen's plundering and raping of Saxon villages. The fierce Vikings did not fear death in battle and enjoyed their recreations. Their long boats brought the king's falcons, as the gyrs were called, so that the marauders might enjoy hawking.

The hawking mania took an even greater hold on England after the advent of the Norman Conquest in 1066. Few men of rank ever appeared abroad without a hawk on their fists. The Saxons spent October and part of December hawking; the Normans flew their hawks throughout the year. Nevertheless, only persons of high rank were allowed to keep hawks, a law that was apparently instituted to restrict hawking privileges to Norman lords and thus reinforce alleged Saxon inferiority.

The Saxons had enthusiasm for falconry, but they did not have style. From the time of William the Conqueror to King John no Saxon was allowed to own a hawk. Finally in 1199, John's barons forced him to allow *all* freemen irrespective of rank to own hawks. John was also the first English king to pass any kind of bird protection law (a factor in its passage, of course, was the necessity for protecting his own hunting rights!).

Sometimes falcons were used to secure estates from the crown, and foreigners used them as a kind of currency. One Geoffry Fitzpierro gave two Norwegian hawks, prized greatly in England, to King John in return for permission for a friend to export a hundredweight of cheese! For the right to travel freely through England, Nicholas the Dane gave the king a hawk every time he visited England.

The Isle of Man, a playground for tourists today, owes its early existence to Sir John Stanley, for Henry IV granted it to him "to be held of the King by homage, and by two falcons presented on the day of the Coronation."

Kenneth III of Scotland rewarded a peasant and his two sons for battle service with "as much land on the River Tay as a falcon cast from a fist would fly over until it settled." The falcon flew six miles, and eventually that land became the estate of the Earl of Errol.

Persons of rank traveled with their hawks. For a "true and valiant knight" to attempt to trade his hawk for his liberty meant loss of honor. Thomas à Becket went to the French Court on embassy for Henry II in the twelfth century, taking with him his hawks and falconers.

On the tombs of knights all over England, the effigy has the knight's dog lying at his feet, his falcon standing on his fists.

In those days, too, falcons had gentler usages than in warfare. Gilbert Blaine says, "the enamoured knight was wont to woo with his hawk on his hand . . . the gift of one of these birds was a pledge between high-born lovers."

Edward III made it a felony to steal a hawk or to take its eggs, punishable by imprisonment up to a year and a day and a fine at the king's pleasure. Lost hawks must be returned to the sheriff. If a hawk thief was caught, he was castrated. When the same King Edward invaded France, he took with him thirty falconers on horseback to care for his hawks.

The past glory of falconry is recorded all over England, but it is in London that the richest heritage is to be found. The city has absorbed tracts of land that were once pre- served for hunting. In Henry VIII's reign, partridges, pheasants, and heron were cultivated from Westminster Palace to St. Giles in the Field, stretching to include Hamp- stead, Islington, and Highgate. It was common to import hawks at high prices (Sir Thomas Moxon, in the reign of James I, gave one thousand pounds for a cast of pere- grines). In Henry's reign fixed dues were paid on landing hawks or herons. The last English monarch to take the field with his hawks was George III.

Today in London, vast numbers of people live in mews that were originally built to house hawks and are now con- verted into luxury houses for the rich. Gleaming cars park in the cobbled passageways where once proud falcons weathered.

In the time of Henry IV a mews stood close to where Charing Cross stands today. Six reigns later the mews was converted into stables. Conversions of this kind took place all over London, where in the heyday of falconry it had been the city of a thousand hawks.

The National Gallery, facing Trafalgar Square, was once the site of the royal mews. In the reign of James I, as well as falcons and eagles (never a Berkut) it held cormorants, for the king enjoyed hunting over the Thames with ospreys and cormorants, and a man called John Wood became the first master of cormorants. After centuries the site became the royal stables, but in the mid-nineteenth century it was taken over and the National Gallery was built on it.

Continental rulers of the Middle Ages were equally passionate about hawks. The great Frederick II of Hohenstaufen, grandson of Barbarossa, was so obsessed by his love of the chase that he once lost an important battle for the sake of a day's hawking.

A falcon on a man's fist, a merlin on a lady's glove, these are the hallmarks of the middle centuries.

Up through the Middle Ages, the falconer held sway. Nothing was done about eagles, probably because it was generally accepted that the great golden eagle of England and Scotland could not be manned. It was thought of as savage, aloof, magnificent, but hardly a sporting possibility.

But because it is the finest and fiercest of birds, it is reasonable to assume that when history attributes great feats to eagles, it considers them all in a class with the Asian Berkut.

In an age where social status defined the hawk one was permitted to fly, only an emperor could fly a Berkut.* A Berkut was so prized by King Wen, ruler of China in 689 B.C., that its food was caught for it by hundreds of other winged hunters and when it died it was given a state funeral. The Japanese Emperor Kwammu had somewhat the same idea. His favorite Berkut enjoyed royal status. It

---

* Social status was clearly defined by the hawk a man was allowed to fly. Only an emperor could fly a golden eagle, though the privilege was seldom, if ever, exercised because of the untamable nature of the eagle; for a king, the gyrfalcon or its tiercel; a prince, the falcon gentle (the common peregrine), and so on down to the holywater clerk who was allowed only a Muskayte (male sparrow hawk), which was small and of little use to a falconer.

sat in the Tokinoma, or secret place, and it too was saved from the "degradation" of killing its own food. Kwammu's hawk trainers, or *takajo*, ranked with the samurai, but their social status was below that of the bird they served. For 2,500 years emperors and shoguns enjoyed hawking, but the sport was confined to the royal household.

As the greatest of all eagles, the Berkut (pronounced "beargoot" in their own lands and "bearcoat" in medieval England) has been desired by emperors as the largest, most savage and temperamental of all raptors, killer of the biggest prey, and therefore the hawk most desirable to subdue. From every Eastern land, civilized when we were savages, there are stories of the hunting prowess of the mighty Berkuts. Alexander the Great, the Chinese and Japanese emperors, and the Russian czars flew them.

Chroniclers claim that Saladin himself owned a wing of Berkuts which he flew against the armored crusaders. These eagles crashed their great wings about the helmeted heads of the knights and their horses; any crusader unhorsed by a Berkut was fortunate to be armored. Lying on the ground, helpless as an overturned beetle, he was at least protected from beak and talons. The story goes that Richard I exchanged three thousand of his eight thousand wing of falcons for one Berkut from Saladin. After that he released Saladin from besieged Acre to show him how to fly his eagle. Often hostilities were halted so that Coeur de Lion, Saladin, and their entourages, could hawk in competition with each other.

Thus, Richard Coeur de Lion became the first English king to own a Berkut.

The next Berkut to be seen in Britain arrived during the

reign of Elizabeth I, more than 400 years later. In an article from *The Field*, August 2, 1890, J. E. Harting writes of the Muscovite emperor who sent the priceless present of a Berkut to the queen. She does not seem to have realized how honored she should have been and gave it scant attention. Possibly the difficulties of reclaiming this eagle and the fact that it was accustomed to hunt wearing a hood and carried on a wooden perch with the end resting in a socket in its master's saddle was all too much for the queen's hawk masters, especially when they were warned that no dogs should be taken on the hunt or they would be destroyed by the Bearcoat, trained as it was to attack wolves. Whatever the reason, the Berkut seemed to become lost without trace during Elizabeth's reign. And it was to remain lost until relatively modern times.

Sam knows the old Chinese books that are the very roots of falconry, and he has read the rich store of English writers in the past centuries: Bert, Blaine, Markham, Latham, Blome, Campbell, and many others. But they are all dead. Sam's intimate knowledge, his *feeling* for falconry, stems from his wide personal experience of all raptors. The complete falconer, and Sam *is* that, knows the subtleties of each species of killer and killed. Without this long apprenticeship in training other birds of prey, Sam could not have manned his Berkut as ably as he has.

Purist falconers speak a language of their own in which hunting birds' feet are called "hands"; their legs, "arms"; and wings, "sails." "Pounces" are a natural for talons, but "petty singles" are somewhat more confusing when used for toes; so probably the layman gets along best by sticking to the words he knows, within limits. For instance, it is unpardonable to call a hunting bird's talons simply "claws."

The practicing falconer must know one small but tricky essential if he is to deal with predators. He must be able to make a falconers' knot, a cunning twist of the leash that can be instantly tied or untied with one hand. An eagle approaching the size of a Berkut is usually perched on her trainer's fist (not wrist); he often has to fasten her to a perch using only his right hand, and he has to be quick and sure in what he does.

Of falconry, Sam writes from his own vast knowledge:

"Many people everywhere have an ambition to learn falconry. Those who try to learn from books never make it. A falconer must be a practicing field naturalist first, only then can he learn falconry from an expert. But who is an expert? In my eyes he is a man who keeps his birds in good condition, winter and summer, and who can hunt them.

"Such people are few; perhaps in Great Britain there are half a dozen. The British Falconers' Club has about two hundred and fifty members. I understand that only five of these actually take game with their falcons.

"Western civilization does not produce people with the necessary qualifications to become falconers. People who live in cities do not understand things as they truly are. A city man at best can, perhaps, make a pet of his falcon; such a bird would be useless to a true falconer.

"The true falconer must handpick his hawk for temper, health, courage, and for hunting its quarry. A short-winged hawk can hunt in wooded country; a long-winged falcon is for open country—if the right prey is there. Almost all birds of prey kept by so-called falconers die within their first year. The death rate of birds of prey is tremendously high even in zoos specializing in keeping them; there are so many diseases that can attack raptors. Add to these the accident rate—a damaged leg, a broken talon, a deformed beak; all these mean death to free-flying birds. Any man flying his hawk at some prey may forget for a moment and fly it at unsuitable quarry or set it an impossible flight. It will, if it is a good bird, battle on until, tired out, it collides with a rock or a tree and is killed.

"I have killed a gos in this way, flying it at a bloody blackbird that was too far away. The blackbird skimmed round a tree, yelling like hell, and my gos hit a tree. It was alive when I found it, but its nervous system was disrupted; it had a fit and died soon after. I'd had it for seven years.

"I killed another gos. This bird had developed keen survival instincts, it was too wise to tackle hares after it had been bumped and kicked by one. In its eagerness to follow a rabbit it hit the ground as the rabbit bolted into its hole. I could have cried. The gos was dead, its legs extended inside the burrow.

"Any death is pitiful and makes me angry. When you carry a falcon, its life is in your hands. So-called falconers come to me complaining, 'I put my falcon out to weather, it was as fit as a fiddle, but when I went to take it up it toppled over, dead.'

"In condition, a falcon is only a few hours away from death; only an expert, knowing his own bird, can judge 'condition' from starvation, even with scales. Yet overfeeding kills as quickly as underfeeding. There are many paradoxes in falconry. I have never lost a bird from underfeeding, but I've lost some through stupidity. To me a dead bird is a dead friend and an autopsy is held so that I may learn not to make the same mistake twice."

All the top birds in falconry fly for the sheer love of it as well as to hunt. For predators in Atalanta's class there remains a reasonable choice of game at which they can be flown. Grouse is the strongest bird on the wing, but pheasants and partridge give good hunting. Rooks, too, are strong and wily game. Carrion crows are pugnacious and powerful and have been known to kill wild hawks flown against them.

However, there are still many birds against which Sam has not flown his eagle. Possibly her most suitable prey would be the kind reserved for the mighty gyrfalcons from Greenland, hawks of endurance and strength, if lacking the peregrine's spirit and dash.

Falcons have dark eyes, but hawks have yellow irises that turn to a deep orange with age and in old age become almost red. Falcons have a notch, or tooth, in their beak for killing and they fly high and hunt their prey by sheer speed and endurance.

In heraldry the falcon is always shown complete with bells, hackles down, beak closed.

The name falcon used to be spelled "fawcon," and it is still pronounced that way. It is derived from the French *fauconnerie,* which has the same meaning but refers to falcons only. In France the word *autoursier* means the man who trains *autout*—others, such as eagles and short-winged hawks. It is rather similar to the meaning of the German *austringer*. The true English translation is "hawker," but it is seldom used today. In England, "falconer" covers the trainers of all birds of prey.

Peregrines have real star quality, their stoop is gloriously dramatic, and they strike their quarry with violence and at a speed of almost two hundred miles an hour. Sam writes: "Some authorities believe that falcons kill with their breastbone, others claim they strike and kill their prey with their hind talon, but I've watched many kills and I believe it is the specially cushioned breastbone that kills. You can hear the wind whistling through the falcon's hard feathers and hear the blow as it strikes. Often their prey is merely stunned and falls to the ground where the falcon's tooth bites through the spinal cord; my observations show this to me very clearly.

"Hawks have no notch, but the legs and talons are more developed than a falcon's of equal size. They can maneuver through trees, and they hunt by stealth, flying in short sprints. They kill by the pressure of their powerful feet, driving needle-sharp talons into their preys' bodies.

"Hawks will not stay manned as falcons will; in fact they're a bloody nuisance in this respect. They are difficult to tame and have to be manned for hours every day. But when they are trained they bring a greater variety of game than the falcons do, and they do not have to be followed for miles over open country."

Eagles outlive men. The Berkuts of Kirghizstan do not die of age; their uncoped beaks grow too long to permit them to eat and they die of starvation. The golden eagle of Scotland often outlives three generations of men. On Sir Archibald Sinclair's estate in Scotland an eagle was certified as one hundred and forty-seven years of age. Near Bruges in Belgium a living golden eagle was certified as one hundred and fifty-three years.

SIX

Animals are not brethren, they are not under-
lings; they are other nations caught with us in
the net of life and time, fellow prisoners in
the splendour and travail of earth.
—Henry Beston

SAM is a Lancashire man. He was born in the town of Horwich (which in old English means White House) at the
foot of a mountain called Rivington Pike, part of the Pen-
nine Chain, known as "the Backbone of England" because
the mountains, hills, and moors make a spine down the center of the country.

In the rebellion of 1745, Bonny Prince Charlie and his
Highlanders marched across the moors as far as Derby before being defeated. Of more immediate importance to Sam
is the fact that he was born in what he calls "the best hawking country in Great Britain." These grouse moors were
the property of the mill owners, and as grouse are the best

prey of all for the noble peregrine falcon, many of the mill owners employed professional falconers.

Horwich itself is a town of steel workers, coal miners, and railway men, whose chief pastime was flying short-distance racing pigeons which were trained to fly over a measured mile to their cotes. The hazel-eyed, blond-headed little Sam flew racing pigeons and won many a sweep against the big, tough men who were his friends. Their life was a hard one, and they would gamble on anything. So very early in life Sam learned to look after himself and to weigh up all the possibilities when he gambled. He learned to lose without flinching and to take winning in his stride. Always his great love was for birds of prey of any kind, and his first chance to learn about falcons and falconry came from a chance encounter when he and his friends were exploring in forbidden places, as boys do.

The owner of Longworth Mills was an almost legendary figure. Except for her servants, she lived alone; it was said that the man she loved was killed in the First World War. She drank hard and rode her horses recklessly, putting them over the stone walls. To the villagers she was a "true lady" but somewhat mad, and she was always known as Madam Longworth.

Madam came unexpectedly onto a gang of boys fishing in her brook. Among them was young Barnes, a slim youngster with blond, curly hair and very blue eyes. That day Madam had been drinking and she carried a whip. The boys were terrified when she cracked it, but they were trapped—the wall was too high to climb.

Against a nearby gate there grew a massive elm, and the

lady challenged the three boys to climb it and told them to hang her white handkerchief on the topmost bough. Two failed, but Sam, slight and wiry and tall for his age, made the climb, much to the lady's astonishment. She chased the other two boys away and told Sam to follow her to the stable, and as they walked she asked questions designed to test his knowledge of animals. Sam trembled with nervousness—all he wanted to do was to go home—but she would not let him go. Instead she offered him a stretch of ground on which were hen-cote mews and cages and told him he could keep anything he liked in them.

So a bargain was struck. Sam became a favorite with the lady, who kept a menagerie of animals and falcons which she looked after herself. Sam would stay until dark among the falcons and the animals, feeding them, cleaning out their cages and mews. In this way, and until Sam was thirteen and went to college, he kept many different animals, birds of prey, and racing pigeons, all under the lady's supervision. Falcons and birds of prey drew Sam like magnets, and he devoured everything he could learn about them. He had falcons and hawks so tame that they would fly free. Sometimes they killed the short-distance racing pigeons. The pigeons' owners knew who had killed them but seldom complained; if they did complain Sam gave them one of his special racing pigeons. Only once tragedy came his way, from a bad-tempered coal merchant. He lured two of the boy's tame falcons through his window and killed them. Sam was heartbroken, and his pigeon-racing friends were incensed on his behalf.

The brutal coal merchant lived to regret it. To the hardened Lancastrians a mate was a mate, right or wrong. On the bowling green of one of the pubs, Sam's champions removed their heavily buckled belts, and the merchant took a terrible beating from Sam's mates.

In the summer Sam spent most of his days out of doors on the moors. He grew to know where to find every breeding bird for miles around. On the mountainous moors a lost man was considered a dead man; mists were very heavy, and even on mistless days a man might simply walk round and round in great circles, getting nowhere. Sam had common sense and instinct, and he could find his way around in the thickest mist. In the hunting season, though he himself disliked guns, he knew exactly where to find the best duck, grouse, and hares.

Falconers and sportsmen from all over the world hunted the moors, and Sam exchanged his knowledge of the terrain for techniques of falconry. While he was a mere child he was flying sparrow hawks at partridges, peregrines at grouse, goshawks at rabbits, and training kestrels for the pure love of it.

When Sam was about ten years old he went with his parents on a holiday to the far north of Scotland. They stayed a few days in Thurso, and Sam went fishing off Scrabster Pier. It was from this pier that Lord Kitchener sailed to his death on the unlucky *Hampshire* during the First World War. On his way back from fishing, Sam noticed a fisherman's cottage. Perched on blocks in front were two of the largest scythe-winged falcons he had ever seen, magnificent birds in lovely plumage.

Through the centuries, the values of hawks have

changed, but those bearing the highest price were the lords of the chase, the Icelandic gyrfalcons. Now Sam was looking at a cast of these wondrous birds.

He was also soon in heated argument, for three Scots boys around his own age, spotting a foreigner, began to taunt him about the Battle of Bannockburn where 30,000 Scots defeated 100,000 English. Warming to their work, they boasted about every battle won by the Scots. Sam, not to be outdone, realized they knew nothing about the battles they had lost. His voice rose to a shriek as he claimed that apart from the Highlanders the rest of the Scots were "arrant scum!"

Words failed them all and Sam set-to with his fishing rod, breaking it on the first boy who came at him. Then all the boys rushed him at once and he fought wildly against odds that were too great for him—when to his astonishment two of the boys were lifted clear of him, their legs treadling as if riding bicycles. Sam looked up to see the biggest kilted man he had ever known.

Laughing deep in his stomach, the big man asked in a broad Highland accent:

"So we're all 'arrant scum,' laddie? Would ya fight Wully here if he'll fight ya? Will ya fight 'im, Wully boy?"

Wully was a squat boy, an inch or two shorter than Sam and with a shock of red hair. Wully nodded his head, and Sam asked the inevitable question any Lancastrian would ask in the same circumstances:

"D'you want to fight fair?"

Sam meant "d'you want a true and honest fist fight, minus feet and gouging?" for in his native Lancashire, clog and other types of fighting took place, and men handsomely allowed their opponents to make their own choice.

Sam fought Wully, of whom he said, "Luckily he was no good, and he jacked it in after a few blows, claiming I'd hurt a nerve in his arm and that I'd been taught to fight in my English school and he hadn't been taught in Scotland."

The giant Scotsman spat his disgust, turned away, and walked into his cottage; he was so tall that he had to stoop to enter the doorway.

The boys went off, and Sam walked home to his tea. But he could not get the memory of the two splendid falcons he had seen out of his mind. He finished his tea and slipped out. He bought some red meat and walked back to the fisherman's cottage. The huge man opened the door, filling it with his thick sweaters and fishermen's boots, and Sam was so frightened he could not speak. Dumbly he held the meat out to him. The Scotsman took it and Sam followed him, watching while he tore up some twine and fed it with the red meat to the giant falcons while Sam looked on in amazement, realizing that the twine would act as a casting.

Addy McLeod was a legend among his people. The huge Highlander was skipper and owner of the largest share in a small motor fishing vessel. He had recently taken his boat out in a gale so fierce that the local lifeboatmen could not put to sea. Addy did the job for them and rescued fishermen drifting in the gale with their stalled engines. Addy McLeod's physique, his natural strength, and his endurance were phenomenal.

To Sam, his mighty kings' falcons were a magnet. He had never seen their kind before, though he had read all about them. He knew that though they were one of the three species of great northern falcons, this cast did not come from Iceland, for the Icelandic gyrs were pure white and these were faintly blotched on closer inspection. But they were splendid nonetheless.

The day after Sam discovered the lovely falcons and crossed paths with Addy, the Highlander, disregarding the objections of his crew, took the boy along deep-sea fishing. Sam knew that if he was a Jonah no other ship in the area would allow him aboard, and he would be considered a Jonah for no greater reason than that the catch was small. Addy also took one of his gyrs aboard, perching it in the wheelhouse where it faced out to sea aloof, elegant and deadly, with its eyes hooded. Sam had bought a gift for his new friend, a peregrine falcon's hood of a design Addy had not seen before. In return Addy took him round the Clett Rock, a cliff away from the mainland on which thousands of seabirds bred and among them a pair of peregrines nested.

Addy pointed out the eyrie to Sam, and the boy left the boat and scrambled up the rock face, returning with a beautiful pair of eyasses (young peregrine eagles) tucked into his shirt. None of Addy's crew would climb and he himself could never leave the wheel, so he was proud of what he called his "spunky English kid."

From that time on, Addy and Sam became fast friends. The Highlander taught the boy from Lancashire many things about the sea and about flying falcons in the mountains. One day he gave Sam a splendid surprise—a clutch of falcon eyasses to take back to Lancashire with him. The young birds were in down, and Addy thought that they were Greenland falcons, for which he knew Sam was longing.

Sam took the eyasses with him when his holiday ended, and when they moulted out they proved to be the pure white Icelandic gyrfalcons! In a few weeks Sam had them flying freely at hack, and they were the tamest falcons he had ever owned and a source of wonderment to everyone who saw them. Then Sam realized regretfully that they had been spoiled by so much kindness and attention; they were so tame that even the pigeon fanciers could bring them down and feed them. But though he had many offers, Sam could not bear to sell them. They were the most superb flyers on the wing, and they brought their own kind of fame to Horwich.

Some years later Sam studied half-time in the Mechanics' Institute, and for the other half he worked to get practice and experience in engineering workshops. He soon realized that however hard he toiled he could not earn money that was adequate for his needs. So he began running a book and found he could make more money in one morning than the average engineer made in a month. The gambler in Sam was balanced by the canny Lancastrian, and he delighted in this. Soon he managed to save £ 800, which he promptly put on a horse in the November handicap, and it won.

So Sam went off and bought a share in Addy's M.F.V. (Motor Fishing Vessel) and he had the happiest six months of his life. During this time with Addy, Sam learned much about falconry from him and from his shepherd and game-keeper friends, including the laird whose salmon they poached in spite of a jealous guard kept by keepers and the river bailiffs as far down river as the last bridge before the sea. Past that it was known as "common water" and anyone was allowed to catch the salmon.

It had been a hot summer and the streams were almost dry. Sam found two young otters in a dry stream; they tamed easily and ate most everything, including bread and milk. They were up to all sorts of tricks and ran free among the poultry, but not being hungry they never touched hens or chickens, although they would steal and eat the eggs of any hen foolish enough to lay away from her nesting box. They were devoted to Addy's family as well as to Sam.

These otters solved the problem of getting the carefully watched salmon into the common water. The otters followed Sam like dogs, each one jealous of the other; Sam trained them to come to a whistle. One day he walked a hundred yards upstream, put the otters in the murky water, then went quietly down below the bridge and blew his whistle. Almost at once the otters, whose sense of hearing is acute, were making large V's in the water, swimming swiftly and silently toward him.

From then on, Sam merely made use of the two sleek swimmers' natural instincts. Wully, Sam's first opponent and now his ally, had large pockets in his sea jacket especially designed for poaching, and he would put an otter in each pocket, releasing them half a mile upriver and then walking away from the bridge, where Sam stood with his whistle.

As the otters swam toward him, Sam saw them driving the salmon before them in play. They were beautiful to watch, swimming with only their noses above water, diving swiftly after any fish that tried to glide beneath them. Thanks to Sam's otters, many a local table was decorated by a salmon, cooked whole, a tomato in its mouth and slices of lemon along its back.

—

Sam had only one unpleasant experience among his fishermen friends. Because of a misconception of the weight of fish consumed by seals—actually seals eat mainly shellfish, crustaceans, and plankton—the fishermen kill any seals entangled in their nets.

The M.F.V. was on her way to the salmon nets when Addy noticed a seal caught in the lines. He fetched the vessel close-by, and to Sam's horror Wully seized a huge gaff hook and struck the seal. Dragging it aboard, he began to batter it with an iron bar. Sam could stand no more. He rushed at Wully who, astonished, struck at Sam with his free left hand. Sam caught it, squeezing Wully's fingers until the boy fell on his knees with tears in his eyes. The crew gathered angrily about them, but Sam was worried only about Addy's reaction; Addy was the law where his boat was concerned.

Addy came swiftly out of the wheelhouse while Sam straddled the badly injured seal which, in its terror, buried its teeth in Sam's leg.

"Ya canna stop Wully—da ya hear me, sonny? Yon seal must die."

"No—Addy, please listen," Sam pleaded. "I'll buy it for ten times the value of its pelt. Anyhow, Wully's ruining its pelt battering it. Why not kill it by pushing a long net needle into its brain?"

This way Sam stalled for time. He knew that in the North sealskins are used for chair covers and slippers and other things. Addy thought Sam's reasoning had some sense to it. A man was sent for the needle and Sam examined the seal to see if its injuries would be fatal. As he turned it over it threatened to snap at his hand and Sam could see the desperate fear and pain in its eyes. It looked up at him beseechingly; its whiskers were dew-spotted with its own blood, its stomach was torn where the gaff had gone into it, and its brown-spotted skull was soft and bloody. It went through Sam's mind to throw it overboard, but it was in no condition to escape. The needle was pushed into his hand. Sam's fingers closed on it and he lifted his arm and threw it overboard, turning to Addy.

"This seal is *not* going to be killed! I'll buy it for any price you name."

Addy looked back at him quizzically, then he answered quietly, "Yon seal eats our living, sonny. What would ya do wi' it?"

"I'll do anything you tell me to. I'll take it with me on Saturday on the *St. Truro* to the Orkneys, or I'll sell it to a zoo or try to keep it as a pet. I've never had a seal before, but I promise it won't touch one of our fish, and I've fifty pounds for the crew if I keep it."

Addy turned his back and walked toward the wheelhouse. Over his shoulder he called, "Gie Wully five pounds, sonny, and yon seal is yours." The crew began to mutter among themselves, but Addy added shortly, "That's an end o' the matter."

Sam gave Wully ten pounds, and in return Wully gave him a leaky old rowboat which Sam filled with sea water and put the seal in it.

It was a common young dog-seal, and a week later it was attracting as much attention as did Addy's falcons. The blows from the iron bar had damaged one eye, so it would never be able to look after itself again. It soon swam for fish such as herrings and was eating mollusks—and even trying Sam's staple, bread and milk!

People bringing food for the seal soon began to pester Addy, so Sam took it to the village of Scrabster. There he rigged a barrel of water on the harbor wall for it. By this time it was as tame as any dog, and the people loved it, so much so that once when a drunken tourist came out of the pub and stubbed his cigarette out on the seal, the enraged locals threw him into the harbor.

Six months later when Sam left Scotland, the seal still lived in its barrel, swam in the harbor, and visited people's houses like any pet. It was a gentle creature and intelligent and was, of course, named Mac. It was also a great lover of the bagpipes, and if the pipe band played on Sunday, the seal followed in the wake of the skirling pipers.

Sam was supremely happy with the companionship of Addy and other men who were a part of this wild, rugged life. Sam learned to prefer wild-caught falcons to eyasses. So many eyasses die because they never learn to kill for themselves. Once a bird is a year old it has developed the knowledge that enables it to survive. There is another wisdom beside killing prey which a parent bird alone can teach—what *not* to attempt in its wild life. All British falconers seem to prefer eyasses, and perhaps that is why so few ever take game with their falcons.

Addy taught Sam a great deal about golden eagles and Sam did his own research. But Addy, in common with the other falconers, would not attempt to train a golden eagle for falconry. He argued that they burned up too much en-

The affectionate Atalanta

Sweet talking Sam

A true bond of friendship was growing

ergy in wing-flapping flight, with which Sam agreed, but Sam also saw that unlike a falcon, whose narrow-tipped wings enable it to fly in very fast pursuit over long distances, the golden eagle in its natural habitat soars and glides at tremendous speeds, and then wing flapping is not needed. An eagle can, at the same time, catch a bird flying at eighty miles an hour and more, and although its big, rounded wings are cumbersome for taking off unless it falls into the wind, its large, strong tail enables it to land and to turn quickly when seizing prey on the ground.

Eagles see their prey from tremendous distances and come after it at great speed, leveling out of the stoop a foot or two above the ground, gliding in with clutching talons at the ready; when hungry they seldom miss.

Sheltering in a cave to which Addy and Sam had followed a wild-cat kitten, the two men watched a golden eagle taking a fox in a raging blizzard. The power and execution of the great eagle fired Sam's imagination, and his desire to train one was born then and there. The eagle's talons went through the fox's muzzle with such crushing force that its eyes burst from its head and the eagle took them with two quick stabs of its beak. Simultaneously in its mad, backpedaling flight, it exerted its thumb and forefinger grip with the back and front talons of each "hand," combining it with such a powerful movement of its legs that the two men heard the fox's spine snap like a stick. One stroke of the eagle's back talons tore the fox's body open, exposing its intestines. Greedily the eagle swallowed a few beaksful before disembowelling the animal completely, thus reducing its weight. Then, facing into the blizzard, the great bird be-

came clumsily airborne, carrying the fox's empty carcass in its talons. No golden eagle, not even the mighty Berkut, could fly carrying a fully grown fox; the heaviest prey Sam has seen Atalanta lift weighed eight and a half pounds.

The Scots, with their great deer forests, guard the golden eagle carefully, and it is to Britain's shame that she has not done so and saved her noblest predator. But even in Scotland, individual shepherds and keepers are still stupid enough to kill them. When this happens and an isolated glen is without its pair of eagles, the young male wanders the glens and mountains of the Highlands like an outlaw, alone, until at maturity it finds a well-stocked hunting range of its own and takes over a domain that is usually about twenty square miles. There it settles down. A female comes along and decides whether this male will make a good provider and mate. The male has no choice.

Sometimes Addy and Sam found an empty glen. Then they would catch a male eagle, perferably three or four years old. Using a long fishing rod with a loop of wire on it, they would snare the eagle when he perched for the night and release him in the chosen glen. Within weeks the females came along, and the lifetime mating with the chosen one would take place. If the men had chosen a female she would have flown away, because it is she who makes the selection.

During Sam's time in Scotland more than three hundred brooding pairs of these magnificent birds were seen and their barking cries were heard through the thin mountain air. Many times Sam watched the dramatic and mysterious courtship rites of the eagles, which take place well above

Atalanta returning to her favorite perch, the stone gatepost
© *"Daily Express"*

the forest timberline. He watched them fall, talons entwined, turning in the air one beneath the other. He saw blood from the male spatter the snow, while his feathers floated down like snowflakes. This aerial display stimulates the eagles, and the real mating takes place on the ground. This is a reason caged eagles do not breed; they lack the necessary midair stimulation.

The golden eagle would be extinct in Great Britain but for the Scottish lairds' deer forests. The Scots must thank James I for the lovely, deep brown, fallow deer that roam through these forests. It was James who had them brought from Norway, the only variety of deer that can withstand the bleakness of the Scottish Highlands.

Occasionally the great eagles take a sickly deer calf, and by so doing they increase the strength of the herd. But the eagles' greatest service to the deer stalker is to prey on the blue hares that ring-bark the trees and remove the cover the stalker needs. This hare, like the ptarmigan and stoat, lives high up in the mountains, almost in the region of perpetual snow. The hares change their coats in winter to pure white, which gives them protection against what is almost their only enemy, the golden eagle.

To understand this great bird, a man must watch it in its natural habitat. He could stare at it in captivity forever and learn nothing. Eagles live where nature is at her most savage, in isolated wilderness where scenery remains unchanged. There the great raptors soar free and are kings. For young Sam, they peopled the solitude. Around him flew plovers and redshanks, ravens and crows, and the dotterel, which breeds at 3,000 feet and over. In the rivers and lochs swam trout and salmon. But his eyes looked upward at the great peaks with their cloud-shrouded tops. Over them he knew the mighty birds of Jove hunted.

After a time Sam's father found him and persuaded him to return home to finish his engineering scholarship. Sam was very reluctant and did so only when he learned that his refusal to complete the training, on which large sums already had been spent, would cost his engineer father his job.

So, reluctantly, Sam went home. Six and a half years in the armed services followed, during which his time in Addy's boat stood him in good stead. In 1944 he was transferred to the Navy and sent to the M.F.V.'s. These motor fishing vessels were powered by Rolls Royce Merlin engines. Sam says, "We could be sounding along the French coast and if a German E boat turned up we either bluffed it out as a fishing boat or we ran for it, and we had the speed to get away. It was great fun."

After the war, his engineering textbooks made him shudder—the only thing he recognized was his own handwriting. Rather than begin learning all over again, he started in business on his own, and he gambled in a big way. Soon he was running three contracting businesses and dealing in marine salvage. His gambling both won and lost him big money, but he always had enough to do whatever he wanted to. Living in towns was a great strain, so he went to live near the mountains and on the seafront at Pwllheli. This way he had his falconry, and he could also join in naturalists' expeditions abroad.

Above everything, Sam is a fine naturalist and a falconer

of endless patience and skill. His own evaluation of himself: "As with everything else I'm only too conscious of being just an amateur. I fly hawks for fun and relaxation and because I want to study and understand their instincts and the brains in those feathered heads. I meet fellow falconers to learn from them, drink with them, enjoy their company. . . ."

The born naturalist needs to know more than recognition and how to handle and care for animals. Sam's interests include folklore, history, botany, medicine and, above all, field work. Only then is Sam able to assess the results of his personal observations.

Sam is by no means a conventional naturalist, getting university degrees; he needs wider horizons. Because of his close cooperation in mammal research with universities and societies all over the world, he is welcomed as a member of any expedition that interests him. The expedition during which he found Atalanta was by invitation; he went as a guest and *Dolmetscher* (translator) to Kirghizstan, where his mountaineering ability was invaluable.

Not everyone likes Sam, the happy extrovert; his thin veneer of civilization can explode in violence and suddenly he is a primitive. But there is the Sam who fills one with wonder at the inexhaustible patience he brings to his craft of falconry and the sentimental Sam with his love of all children.

Ron Semmens, a falconer whom Sam trusts and who helps him fly Atalanta, recalls the first time he saw Sam. Ron was a corporal in the Queen's Royal Hussars, based in Germany:

"I was in the Navy, Army, Air Force Institution Club,

watching a football match on television. It was for the German Meisterschaft. As it was half-time, both teams were off the field. Suddenly, over a protective dike and onto the running track around the field jumped a tall figure in flannels and an open-necked white shirt. As he began his sprint round the track, the crowd of 120,000 went wild with the whistling that takes the place of cheering in Germany. In the man's right hand was a banner on a stick which said *Grüsse aus Gross Britannien nach Deutschland* (Greetings from Great Britain to the Germans) , and on his left fist a falcon stood with extended wings. Policemen, firemen, and ambulance men closed in, but the tall figure simply passed through them, side-stepping like a rugby player. One policeman dived, he missed the quickly moving figure but managed to grab the banner. The German waiter serving us stood staring at the screen and muttering *Er is kein Engländer!* (He is no Englishman!)

"Some days later the wine festival began. This goes on for days—and nights. There are fairgrounds, a circus, much drinking, and everyone enjoys himself. I went with a squad of my soldier-pals to the Game Fair, where the falconry championships were held; a fascinating pageant with falconers in livery from all over the world. Because I've always been especially interested in them, we went to watch the eagles fly.

"That day the eagles were to be flown at deer freed from a pen. An Austrian falconer went first, his fawn-colored golden eagle on his fist. He unhooded his eagle; then he spent ten minutes removing the rest of its equipment before shouting *Fertig!* (ready) to the forester who opened the pen and released the deer. It sped downwind and across

Free

flight

open ground, making for the undergrowth of the nearby pine forest. The falconer had to throw his eagle downwind, causing the big bird to fall to the ground after flying ten yards, then it ran with beating wings before it could be airborne. The deer escaped and the eagle took stand in a tree, much to the amusement of the crowd.

"Six falconers representing their different countries had rather similar experiences and we became bored; none of the eagles caught the deer. Then it was the turn of the seventh falconer. As he appeared, the German crowd went mad and shouted: *Unserer Engländer! Die schwarze Jägerine!* (Our Englishman! The black huntress!)

"To my astonishment this man was the same open-necked, white-shirted figure which had run around the football pitch the day before! He wore no plumed hat covered in badges, no fancy livery—not that it is likely that anyone would have noticed, for all eyes were on the magnificent eagle on his fist, unhooded, untethered except for her jesses. What a massive, splendid creature she was, she was also nearly black in the sunlight.

"The Englishman walked stiff-legged, and his red, sun-browned face suggested a few cognacs. When he reached his stand he shouted immediately, *Fertig!* The forester was so amazed at the speed that he failed to open the pen and the Englishman swore at him in German, saying he would release his eagle at *him* because she was too heavy to hold much longer! The Germans loved it. It appeared the eagle was famous to these West Germans; later I learned she was said to have taken one of the hated East Volk-Polizei through the throat.

"The forester released the deer. To the wonderment of

the crowd, the Englishman turned his back on the running deer and held the massive black eagle into the wind. She flapped away for three or four wingbeats in the opposite direction, while the Englishman began running toward the deer. The crowd laughed loudly and called him stupid, shouting, *Er ist ganz verrückt!* (He is quite mad!) But a world-famous falconer standing next to me said to his friend, *Auf-passen, er ist nicht verrückt!* (Watch carefully, he is not mad at all.)

"Suddenly the eagle held her great wings at full stretch and shot up into the wind, banking round as she did so. This allowed her to stoop into the wind at a very fast speed to cut off the deer. She hit the deer with such a thud that all the watchers heard it. A forester dashed up with his knife. As he was going to plunge it into the crazed beast's throat, a foot hit his hand, knocking the knife flying. It was the Englishman. The forester sprang up in a rage and made for the Englishman who, laughing, threw something through the air. The German caught it deftly—it was the Englishman's flask—and the German drank from it heartily.

"The white-shirted figure bent down. His gloved fist was baited with raw meat; he hit it against the eagle's strong legs. The eagle obediently stepped off the deer and onto the man's fist and began to pull at the meat. The deer got to its feet and made for the safety of the pine trees.

"A commotion broke out among the officials, but the Englishman was obviously not interested; the crowd loved every second of it. As he walked through the excited officials 'disqualified,' the eagle nibbled and pulled at his tousled blond hair; obviously she was as unworried as was her master.

"When I was discharged from the Army I came to Wales, married a Pwllheli girl, and discovered that Sam Barnes lived there with his *schwarze Jägerine*."

SEVEN

There is something very dreadful, so satanic,
in tormenting those who have never harmed
us and cannot defend themselves.
—CARDINAL NEWMAN

IN contrast to the early days of unceasing battle with the
Berkut, the days that followed were truly happy ones. For
Sam they represented the all important period of manning,
getting the bird used to handling, teaching her to trust her
master under all circumstances—and trust remains a tenuous thread for a long time before a hawk reaches her final
decision.

During the days that followed their battle, Sam carried
his eagle the whole day long in spite of her great weight. At
night she slept peacefully on her screen perch in the bay
window of Sam's bedroom. He gave her plenty of good
food, and that alone made her more amiable toward him.

Many problems remained to be solved, but Sam had a

full measure of delight in watching the royal creature as she played on his lawn. For the first time Sam watched the grotesque abandon of a Berkut becoming kittenish, and he found it endearing. She pursued a plastic ball like some waddling old duck. Sometimes he gave her a full-sized football to propel about the lawn, but neither plastic ball nor football lasted for more than a few minutes under her assaults; no plaything could stand up to those piercing talons when she meant business. Several times a day, as she paused panting from her exertions, she would suddenly remember her bath and go and cool off while Sam sprayed her with a strirrup pump.

The groups of spectators outside the fence never dwindled. At first newcomers were filled with amazement at the size and beauty of the Berkut. Then she would blow out all her feathers like something suddenly charged with electricity and squat in her bath like any fat duck, filling it with an overflow that kept the grass bright green around it.

There is nothing halfhearted about an eagle taking a bath. Once it is in its bath, it is just a little more ludicrous than the eagle on the ground. She would splay her tail and move her closed wings vigorously. Then she reversed. Finally she wriggled her head under the water like some alarming snake. During all this clownish performance, Sam went on spraying her until she looked more like a wet mop than a proud eagle.

When she had gone through all the motions, she jumped out and shook herself like a dog. Then, comfortably cool, she lay on the lawn, spreading her great wings to dry while she sunbathed. To measure her wingspan, Sam put a teaspoon at the tip of each wing where the longest feather

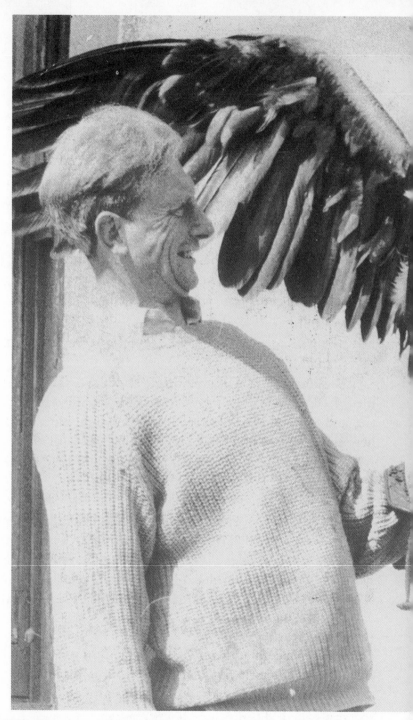

What better companion could any man wish for? © *Jack Smith*

grew and measured the distance between the spoons. The distance was well over eight feet—she was a young bird then. Since then the span has increased to about nine and a half feet.

By now it was the middle of August, and Sam's wounds had become scars. His beloved bird grew tamer with the days, until he could even play with her. Sometimes when she was feeding, he would pretend to take a running kick at her, but by then she was so sure of herself and of him that she completely ignored it.

It seemed to Sam that the miracle for which he had always hoped was gradually taking place and a true bond of affection was growing between them. Cautiously, he told himself the "eagle is an unpredictable bird." It can be moody and suspicious one day, childlike and absurd the next. The Berkut was always likely to resent liberties on her off days; at those times he must not touch her prey or her food or prod her off the window ledge to clean beneath her. Such liberties brought on a display of raised hackles, open beak, visible tongue, spread talons—the classic stance of the heraldic eagle always shown "armed."

One sultry August day Sam went for a swim on a less crowded beach across the promenade. The water was cool and the afternoon quiet. Sam was rocking gently in the cool sea, when the stillness of the afternoon was rent by the loud revving of a number of motor scooters in the distance. Wrapped in his own thoughts and lapped by the gentle ripples, Sam was unconscious of the racket, which was the sound of a leather-coated gang that had arrived to see the eagle.

Spectators seem to smell trouble the way a vampire

smells blood; they soon crowded against the low stone wall between the lawn and the Parade where the eagle was playing happily. The motorcycle brigade began to taunt the tied bird, revving up their engines, throwing lighted cigarettes at the by now crazily bating eagle. The scooters exploded with a shattering noise. The gang leader, determined to prove himself, vaulted the wall with two of his cronies at his heels, picked up an oar, and prodded the terrified eagle. The leader made a dash for her block and cut through the creance with his jackknife.

The Berkut took off like a rocket, zooming across the Parade and the crowded beach, with fifty yards of nylon creance trailing after her. A roar went up from the crowd, followed by a kind of mass hysteria as most of them panicked.

In a few minutes four and a half miles of crowded beach was emptied of holiday makers. Someone rushed into the water and swam out to where Sam was unconscious of these goings-on. When he heard what had happened he made for the shore, ran out of the water and across the Parade, wearing only his bathing shorts.

Inwardly Sam raged against the senseless cruelty inflicted on his bird, and he was terribly afraid for her. The motorscooter gang was leaving, but the gang leader was the last to start. Sam raced after him. As he roared away, Sam stooped, picked up a stone, and hurled it after him. It caught the lout on the back of his neck, sending the scooter careering across the road and crashing into the Parade railings, head on. The boy went over the railings like a wet sack. By the time he remounted, Sam was half a mile down the beach, his whole mind set on reclaiming his eagle.

Fear did not confuse the Berkut's intelligence. She passed over the beach in level flight for about a mile and then spiraled up into a pitch from which she could survey the situation. On one side of her was a motor-filled road and a crowd of moving people; on the other side the shining, ever-moving sea stretched to the horizon. She did not like either view. She turned, stretched her great wings, and soared back along the deserted beach.

Sam sighed with relief when he saw his eagle flying toward him out of the distance; she moved in a glide over his head and it seemed to him that the great copper-shining wings dipped in salute.

Sam had snatched up his gauntlet; he had no whistle. He was sure the Berkut recognized him, but the situation was alien to her and she was uncertain what to do. She spiraled up and branched off at a tangent, then turned toward Snowdon, twelve miles away and the tallest mountain in England or Wales, rising above the vast Snowdonian Range where, according to the Welsh, King Arthur once lived in a cave guarded by eagles.

This was a dreadful moment for Sam. He stood in an agony of suspense, groaning; he could only stand helplessly by. Holding her wings motionless, she glided across the beach and over the Parade. Suddenly as he watched he saw her wings become taut, she swooped down and landed on the flat roof of a pink house owned by a retired businessman.

From her high perch on the roof the Berkut surveyed the moving throng of people who seemed to have appeared from nowhere to watch her. Fortunately, the owner of the house was a man with a cool head and plenty of common sense. Right then he was the hero the hour needed, and Sam begrudged him none of the crowd's acclaim. With great courage he seized the dangling creance and held on to it until the panting falconer arrived. Sam pulled her down and took her on his fist.

For the first time Sam was able to look around him, and he found that the crowd had caught up with them. People were so closely packed about him that he could not force his way through. The eagle's behavior was cool and disinterested. Sam got the impression that she was glad to return to him. Cameras, like ugly black flowers, blossomed everywhere. Then the crowd thinned enough for the man and his eagle to return home.

Within an hour, the Berkut was back on her block, preening herself, keeping one veiled but fierce eye on an audience which watched her admiringly—from a safe distance.

Next day the national press used such headlines as SWOOPING TERROR SCATTERS CROWD, but Sam noticed that they printed no condemnation of the motorcycle gang's cruel behavior. The local police arrived. Pwllheli is a center of Welsh nationalism, and it seemed that because Sam is English and his eagle is a foreigner, both their heads must roll. This was the first of many incidents involving the law that were to plague Sam. But they certainly caused no concern to his eagle.

In spite of much to-do, it was decided that no offence had been committed, though a visiting official did say, "If that dangerous creature comes near me, I'll—I'll strike it down!" Which amused Sam because in the same issue of the paper there were photos of "the dangerous creature" being stroked by children. Then some legal light decided that the onus was on the police to prove the eagle dangerous, not on Sam to prove it safe. Possibly the decision was related to the fact that hotel proprietors knew that the eagle was a fine publicity gimmick for them.

The motor-scooter incident had one important consequence: it made Sam realize that he must try to shorten the training period, which meant less than the normal six weeks to two months before she would be ready for free flight. Sam decided to attempt free flights in exactly four weeks.

Free flying is a serious problem, and Sam discussed it with his neighbor Griff Thomas, who was fascinated by the great bird and wanted to be one of her chief handlers so that he could take over from Sam whenever he was away. They discussed the various methods of flying the eagle. She could be flown tethered by hundreds of yards of nylon creance from a large fishing reel, but there was the risk of injury if she had to be dragged down. She was well fed and "high" in condition, but not in the state a falconer requires before he flies his hawk. For this she should be "sharp set" and "keen on" with hunger pangs; then the trained bird will come to the fist for food.

So they ruled out this method; besides, when she was trained, Sam expected her to come to his fist because she herself wanted to, not just for food. This bond of love, not hunger, between master and bird is the mark of the good falconer.

Sam knew that in the early stages of training, his Berkut,

because she retained her natural power of flight, might if sharp set with hunger pangs fly into the mountains and make her own kills in a wild state.

Sam's ace in training was that an eagle, well-fed and high in condition, would not fly away to hunt food, because eagles kill from hunger and not, as with man, for killing's sake. Both Sam and Griff Thomas agreed that his bird might not return to his fist but that she had been so well manned that when she landed he would be able to take her up, providing he could find her.

Thorough manning can make the difference between a lost and a reclaimed hawk, and the Berkut was well-manned so far. It was asking too much of her to fly her over the open, crowded seafront or above people and traffic and expect her to return to her favorite perch, the stone gatepost of her home. What they needed was a secluded and, if possible, enclosed space for this first free flight.

An airing out

EIGHT

Demetrius directed every man to say his prayers before going hawking. —BLAINE, 1840

AFTER a search, Sam and his friend found a good spot for a trial free flight. It was down by the Talcymerau River, an open space flanked on either side by an avenue of trees. About twenty yards in front of a wall stood a tree stump which made a fine landing perch for an eagle.

Sam took the Berkut to the stump and, stroking her gently, his face close to the fierce head, he crooned to her until he knew she was at ease. Then he carried her away and, holding her creance, flew her back to the stump, varying the distance every time, always careful not to alarm her.

It was Griff Thomas' turn. He flew her while Sam called to her. It was strange country to the big bird, and Sam wanted her to feel reassured before he removed her creance.

The sight of the familiar, tall, fair-haired figure gave the golden bird the confidence to land on the tree stump rather than on Sam's fist.

Sam felt a great exhilaration seeing the massive spread of wings as she came toward him, then her braking flight by backpedaling her wings and splaying her tail before landing neatly on the stump. For the last series of flights she used the full fifty yards of creance.

Now both men felt the time had come to risk a free flight.

Sam removed the Berkut's furniture, and she perched without creance and without the realization that she was free, free as when she had been a wild eagle flying among the towering mountains of the Tien Shan. Sam took her up on his fist and walked a couple of hundred yards from the stump, while Griff Thomas positioned himself between the stump and the high wall.

This positioning was Sam's mistake. He should have stood near the stump and let his companion fly the eagle —something he did not realize at the thrilling moment when he heard Griff Thomas's whistle and threw the great feathered body to freedom.

The Berkut rose from Sam's fist with ponderous wing-beats and flew at a deceptive speed toward the stump. But it was not her master that she saw. Kek-kek-kekking in alarm, she screamed harshly and flew over the stump, turning in a right-hand curve and going away. Sam's heart kicked over at her cries of alarm. She was in imminent danger. If she broke the cover of the trees with her great wingspan— Sam felt sick at the thought.

Her shrieks piercing the clear air, she went through the

trees, scattering dead branches and twigs in all directions. By some miracle, she made it through the trees—and flew on toward the horizon. Her harsh screaming grew fainter and she disappeared from sight.

Sam stood where he was, utterly lost. He saw Griff Thomas sitting down calmly and lighting a cigarette. Griff tried to comfort Sam; they both knew it would be waste of time to search for the Berkut immediately. Trained hunting birds have a strange habit of returning to the place from which they were originally flown.

For more than two hours the men sat watching the horizon. Sam's eyes grew tired and played tricks with him. A dark shape appeared against the sky, far beyond the fields that stretched before them.

Neither man moved as the dark shape came nearer. It was the Berkut. She came in at the terrific burst of speed that was characteristic of her mountain flight and then zoomed in to a stoop, landing on a dead branch about two hundred yards away.

Sam could scarcely believe it—the golden bird had returned of her own accord. It had been a dreadful two hours, filled with visions of farmers with guns, of lethal wire fences. His bird's next moves filled him with delight. She began to bob about, moving her head excitedly, all the time uttering low, far-carrying calls. It was a chattering, songlike noise, and it seemed directed at her master, as if she were asking to be taken up!

Sam reclaimed his hawk, and a short time later the interrupted lesson began again—this time with the creance tied to the stump. Before the men called it a day, the Berkut made three two-hundred-yard flights to Griff Thomas at the stump.

Within four weeks Sam had trained the mightiest of hunting birds to fly free. Sam, who had already trained three kestrels to return to his fist after three days' training, believed it a world record, seconded only by a clergyman in 1854 who taught a sparrow hawk to fly free in ten days' training. The time had come when Sam decided his eagle must be given a name. From his vast knowledge of eagle legends he had narrowed the choice to the two great huntresses of mythology, Atalanta and Diana. Diana, Virgin Goddess of the Moon, was the simpler name, but Diana represented chastity, which seemed inappropriate for the mother of two for whom Sam meant to find a new mate in the future.

Atalanta sounded rather clumsy, he thought, watching his bird preen herself in the sunshine. He considered the implications of the name. According to the myth, the fleet-footed she-devil, the huntress of Arcadia, abandoned by a father who wanted a son and suckled by a she-bear, Atalanta, Goddess of the Hunt, would yield only to the god who could prove himself fleeter of foot than she. Many gods failed in the race and died before Aphrodite gave Meilanion the three golden apples of the Hesperides. Cunning Meilanion dropped the apples during the race and won when Atalanta, Goddess of the Hunt, paused to pick them up. The goddess and the Berkut had much in common: beauty, savagery, speed—and final capitulation to the chosen one.

Still Sam would have deferred the naming, but spectators by his wall began calling the proud eagle Pretty Polly and children named her anything from Alfred to Sebastian.

© *North Wales Press*

Then the name was chosen in what Sam considered an appropriate manner.

A repertory company came to see the eagle and to enjoy the publicity they received from posing with her. Among the visitors were three young actors vying for the favor of a handsome girl in the company. Sam decided the rivalry by inducing the three would-be lovers to race the Berkut—losers to jump in the sea with their clothes on, winners to stay dry and win the lady.

Sam replaced the Golden Apple with a strategically placed rabbit leg to which Atalanta raked off, and the last suitor romped home the winner. The matter was settled, and Atalanta was named.

NINE

*An eagle is trained by using instinct rather
than intelligence.* —SAM BARNES

SAM moved in bed; Atalanta on her screen perch tensed at
once and turned her austere head to stare at him. He did
not stare back; wild eagles resent being stared at. He rose
and walked quietly across the room and began to dress. As
Sam became more the self she knew in manner and dress,
she calmed down, watching him from under frowning
brows.

She had been unhooded all night to accustom her to
every sight and sound around her. Her hood was one article
of furniture that Sam hoped to discard as soon as possible.
The screen perch limited her movement by the length of
the jesses. The leash was pulled and tied through a slit in
the double-hung screen, so that the swivel was rigidly tight

Daily weigh-in—twenty six pounds

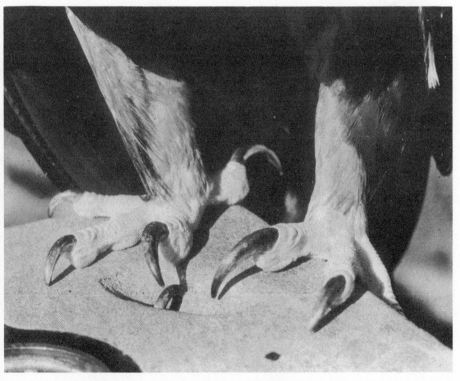

A variety of perches keeps Atalanta's feet trim

Food is a matter of quality not quantity

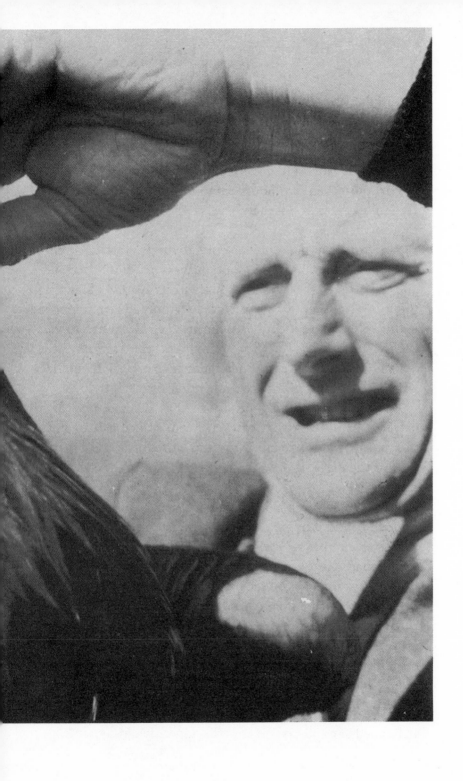

at the top of the pole yet free to revolve. This is the safest way to tether such a huge bird on that type of perch.

For more than two hours Sam moved quietly about near Atalanta. She was alternately relaxed and suspicious of his movements.

Sam touched her golden head lovingly, talking gently and persistently until her nervousness gradually left her and he stroked her great talons with a feather. Standing there, wooing her, Sam was conscious only of her splendor —the splendor that must have caused Shakespeare to call eagles "birds of Jove." Sam's thoughts were concentrated on the tenuous thread of confidence between them. He willed her to trust him as he made his decision.

At first Atalanta did not realize that she was free. Sam baited a gauntlet with a chicken head, splitting it to show the brains, and stretched the garnished gauntlet slowly toward the eagle. Would she strike? Or would she accept his tribute?

With a "kek-kek-kek" of halfhearted anger, Atalanta stepped confidently onto the outstretched gauntlet and tore at her chicken head. Sam's delight was short-lived, for no sooner had she eaten the head when she realized she was free and would not be set back onto her screen perch. Instead she jumped onto the bed head.

Sam had been prepared for her to rampage around the room; from the perch of her choice, now surveying him disdainfully, he realized this could be the prelude to a tough encounter. Fortunately his concern was groundless. Quietly, he moved beside her. When she gave no trouble, he hooded her and carried her triumphantly downstairs.

The day itself seemed to celebrate his triumph. He stood holding his powerful bird close to his shoulder, drinking in the fresh tang of the salty air, hearing the swish of the waves, and in a few minutes he set her on her butcher's block and long-tied her and removed her hood.

While strange sights and sounds could still cause her to bate badly, Sam no longer used the bar bell and weights; she could fly to the edge of the lawn on the creance. Sam wanted to keep Atalanta pleased to see him, and to that end he would offer her tidbits from the gauntlet, taking care to keep his hand lower than her beak. If he dropped his hand, she might be tempted to rake at it with her deadly talons. So that she would associate sound with food, Sam preceded the offer of some special trifle—"bechins," the falconer calls them—by blowing his whistle.

When late that evening Sam took Atalanta onto his fist, carried her up to his room, and put her on her screen perch, he was pleased to see that she accepted the transfer from fist to perch without a sign of bating.

Next morning Sam put Atalanta out to weather about eight o'clock. Then he went around to the back of the house where he has his private zoo. One of his rabbits lay dead, apparently mauled by a cat. Sam thought he knew the killer—a tom belonging to a neighbor who fed it well but let it roam at will until it became a semiwild hunter. Sam often found it lurking around his zoo, taking any bird or small animal it could kill. When Sam complained, the owner remarked that it was a cat's nature to hunt.

Deciding to make the best of a bad job, Sam removed the entrails from the rabbit and gave it to Atalanta. He

was indoors washing up when, to his amazement, who should saunter across the lawn but the marauding tom. It stopped by the little heap of entrails, sniffed them gloatingly, yawned, and licked its lips. Glancing about, it bent its head and picked out the liver and carried it under the privet hedge.

With a speed not even a cat could rival, Atalanta reached the tom. One of her great black talons crushed the cat's ribs, while the other drove deep into its brain. The nervous jerking of the dead cat made the eagle tighten her grip until the back talon met the front in each great foot.

Luckily it had become a showery day and there were few people about; Sam was the only witness to the killing. If the truth must be told, Sam could not regret what Atalanta had done: he had lost too many gentle birds and mammals to wish the killer a longer life to prey on them. He allowed Atalanta to plume and to eat her fill of the cat before putting the remains into a bag and carrying them to the beach to bury under a sand dune, thinking to himself how true it was that "all they that take the sword, shall perish by the sword."

Probably orthodox austringers would have been horrified by the way Sam broke the accepted rules and regulations of the British Falconers' Club with his deviant training methods over the three days that followed. Now the different aspects of training began to emerge, the taming, the calling to the fist. Sometimes the eagle stepped unhesitatingly onto his fist—and then began to bate violently upsidedown, struggling under his aching arm.

Patience, patience must be used at all times, especially

when things go badly for no apparent reason; but what he really longed to do was to shake the living daylights out of the stupidly flapping creature on his arm! It was especially difficult to hold onto his self-control when her heavy wings hit him exasperating blows across his face—blows solid as the jabs of a heavyweight boxer—while Atalanta struggled to take flight.

Every day Sam and his eagle walked together; his tired muscles took the weight of the great silent presence on his fist, but his mind held only one hope: that she would train quickly and release him from this bondage. Today he might be hopeful, tomorrow despairing, for no man can predict an eagle's behavior.

For their first walks Sam and his eagle went by the light of the street lamps. In this way Atalanta gradually learned to tolerate people going about their daily tasks: painters shifting their ladders, milkmen rattling bottles, those and all the other noises she had to learn to endure away from the security of her own lawns. During these first walks, one thing after another caused bone-wearying battles between them. Sometimes for long stretches of time Sam felt that there was just nothing, no advance—stupidity and failure for them both.

One morning Sam finally lost all optimism; even after a short rest it did not return as usual. Worse still, he began to doubt his ability to train and hunt this Goliath of a bird. He ached in every limb and his mind was black with depression. He remembered that T. H. White had felt the same way during the training of Gos, his goshawk; he too had had this feeling of loss, of the bird going away from him emotionally, and this master of words (if not of falconry) had written: "The essence of falconry is not the flight or the kill, but man's relations with his hawk."

Sam's relations with his hawk were at their lowest ebb; he was tired and confused, a condition reflected by Atalanta's remoteness. Perhaps he should give the Berkut to a zoo with a large aviary?

On Saturday evening Sam walked across the fields behind his house with the eagle on his fist, as he always carried her. He felt the increased pressure of the iron talons as the Berkut's frowning eyes traced a flock of curlews across the crimson-tinted sky. Curlews, with their peculiar call, are strong fliers. Few British birds can equal their speed and power of flight and Sam loved to watch them. But now he had eyes only for the beautiful, maddening heavyweight creature on his fist. What better companion could any man wish for? He lifted his free hand and touched the satiny feathers of her broad chest. It excited her when Sam ran his fingers up and down her breastbone, and she opened her breast feathers. Sam twisted his fist to make her open her wings and spread her tail to balance herself. Thus could he admire her from all sides, take note of any broken or bent feathers. Suddenly life seemed calm and lovely, and the tie between master and bird less tenuous than it had been.

Sam looked her over carefully, deciding to imp her broken feathers which would then renew themselves during the next year's moult. The bent feathers he would straighten by dipping into hot water. . . . He walked on. Would she be difficult about it? Unless her feathers were kept in trim, her flight power would be impaired.

They reached the turnpike leading to the main road, and the Berkut seemed to go mad. It was as if she had never seen traffic before. She bated, hung upside down, and refused to climb back. Sam struggled with her as the evening breeze sprang up, but he could not face her into the wind. It seemed that their new-found companionship was shattered, and for no reason he could understand.

The objective of the walk was an open refuse pit in which Atalanta had been scheduled to undergo a kind of ordeal by fire. Sam believed if he carried her through the burning pit without injury it would build her confidence in him.

The refuse pit lay downwind; it was impossible that she had sensed what he had in mind, yet Sam could not quiet her. He broke his own rule and threw her back onto his fist again. Again she bated deliberately; he put her back; she bated, and he left her upside down, flapping wildly like some grotesque and giant bat. He tried every trick known to austringers; no use.

On each side of them the road became blocked by slow-moving cars filled with curious people. The eagle's maniacal rage made Sam even more determined to go through with his plans. With aching arms he carried her, still hanging and flapping, and flopped her down onto the stinking refuse pit. It had taken them seventeen minutes to cover that final hundred yards.

Utterly exhausted, disappointed, and infuriated, Sam dropped beside the unrepentant bird and pulled her back from all the filth to where she perched, panting on his fist. When he got his breath back he looked at her closely, fear-

Atalanta and Shep

ing her finely balanced temper might be ruined by some nervous strain sending her into a fit. Nervous strain can turn birds of prey into lunatic things, forever ruined for the free flying, free hunting life for which Sam was trying to fit Atalanta. He summoned all his experience and watched for these malign signs, but except for the rapid panting he could find no other trace of weakness.

Sam began to worry, knowing that he had lost control of himself as far as he dared while still being conscious of his bird's safety. He knew that mad periods of bating, which were a kind of intermittent insanity, sometimes came to female eagles. Then he decided that Atalanta was playing with him, seeing how far she could go—a technique not unknown in the females of other species.

After the eagle calmed down, Sam sat and considered what he would do. His mind made up, he rose: this was to be the big test. Strong winds whipped the open, smoldering pit into a furnace. Facing the Berkut into the wind so that she balanced on taut, outstretched wings, Sam walked forward into the smoke and flames.

For nearly half an hour there was pandemonium. Screaming as she had on her arrival at Pwllheli, Atalanta settled down to fight him. Sam believed she was well aware he would not allow her to be hurt, and at the first entry he proved this by refusing to let the smoke and flames touch her. She bated in a nonstop flurry. Sometimes Sam had to rest his arm by letting her hang downward, her head cocked stiffly, twisting slowly around and around on her jesses. She could have climbed back onto his fist, but she would not. If he threw her up, she came upright like a wooden puppet, refusing to grip with her talons and toppling down again; nor would she flap her great wings when he flicked his wrist and tried to induce her to throw back onto his fist for herself.

In falconry, as in everything else, there is always the chance of making a wrong move. An inner voice told Sam to go ahead with this ultimate ordeal by fire as he had planned, so that he and the eagle would go through it together and she would know once and for all that she was safe in his hands. Many times during that half hour of torture he doubted his own wisdom, but by then it was too late to turn back.

Finally Sam came to the point of exhaustion, and he believed that Atalanta was exhausted too. Thirty long minutes went by before he sat down and let the fresh wind blow on them both like a blessing.

Now that Sam was still, the mighty Berkut balanced on his fist and watched him with fiercely unrepentant eyes. Her beak was agape, her tongue protruded like the tongue of an exhausted dog. Gradually the coolness of the evening wind brought her high temperature down, and with it went the ill-humor of bird and master. They began their homeward trek.

That evening, she flew the length of the lawn three times, straight onto Sam's fist to get the chicken heads held in the gauntlet. After the horrors of the long day, Sam was so enraptured by her performance that all his optimism returned; with weary joy he knew that while he had not vanquished the great bird, neither had she broken his endurance. In his imagination he saw her, trained to perfection, riding the thermals down from the mountains, and he cracked a bottle of scotch to celebrate.

That night the Berkut cast, so next day she was hungry and once again in an obstinate mood. She refused to fly to the fist, and Sam had to be satisfied to let her step up onto the gauntlet.

Her sudden obstinacies baffled him and also made him anxious. He decided to break his training schedule by refusing her either tidbits or her daily gorge. His idea was to make her sharp set, to have her so hungry she would fly at once to his fist.

This proved to be a mistake.

A day or so later, with his eagle out on the lawn to weather, two schoolteacher friends of Sam's arrived. One of them, Ed, was a keen bird man; Arnold, an art teacher, painted birds. Of course both men wanted to see Atalanta fly to the fist. Sam baited the gauntlet with rabbit's liver, and to everyone's astonishment she hurled herself at her trainer's fist even before he could blow the predinner blast on his thunderer whistle. When Sam put her down, he threw her a piece of rabbit, which she caught in her talon in midair like a cricketer fielding a ball.

"Could a stranger call her to the fist?" Ed asked.

"I think so. She comes to me freely enough, but then I'm with her day and night. I expect you noticed I put her down at once. She may be aggressive, she has hunger pangs."

That was enough warning for Ed but not for Arnold. Sam had put down his gauntlet and whistle to go indoors for a moment and thus did not see Arnold put on the

gauntlet and advance into the territory the eagle considered
her own. When he was still about twenty yards away, Arnold turned and faced the Berkut, held out his gloved fist,
and blew the whistle.

Atalanta lowered her austere head and then moved it like
a snake at the beginning of its strike. Arnold's second blast
Sam heard and rushed to the door in time to shout, "Turn
your back to her, you bloody fool! She'll knock you flat if
you try to take her up facing you!"

Falconers always turn their backs to their hawks; other-
wise the bird lands on the fist facing the wrong way and the
man will be buffeted by the wings. Sam's warning was too
late. It is quite an experience to see an eagle as powerful
and as heavy as Atalanta coming head on, and it was an experience Arnold could have done without. In his desperation he tried to run backward, but the Berkut, irritated by
her hunger pangs, and perhaps by her recent flight to her
master's fist to receive so meager a reward, flew arrow-
straight at the interloper.

The onlookers were speechless and Ed stood shouting
with laughter, as Arnold threw up an arm to protect his
face—which was as well, for the inside talon of the big foot
tore down his arm and the other raked out and gripped his
sport jacket. Atalanta clung on like this until the momentum of Arnold's backward stagger reached the end of the
creance and he hit the wall minus a lump of his jacket and
did a well-executed back somersault over the low wall.
When he reappeared on the lawn, neither of his friends
gave him any sympathy; although he was whitefaced and
shaken, he was unhurt.

The three friends were still laughing over drinks at

Arnold's initiation into falconry, when a howling and yelping came from the lawn. They rushed outside to find a
crowd staring over the wall. A group of youngsters who had
been catching rats at the refuse pit, and had seen the terrified Berkut's efforts to escape the fire misunderstood her
capabilities; one of them owned a shaggy Welsh terrier
which was an efficient ratter, so they thought they would set
it at the Berkut.

The spunky little terrier ran toward where the eagle was
perched. Atalanta's fierce eyes shone with their killer's fire
as the game dog hurled itself at her. The eagle went back
on her splayed tail and raked at the airborne terrier with
both sets of talons. One set missed; the other touched the
terrier without getting a grip. The unfortunate dog landed
on the ground yelping its agony. It got up and tried to
streak back over the wall to safety, but now the big raptor
had a quarry. With outstretched wings she bounded after
the pitiful little beast, which had no chance at all of escaping her.

Fortunately the Berkut took the terrier through its
hindquarters and dragged it, alive and howling, toward her
shelter at the bottom of the lawn. There she intended to
kill and eat the dog at her leisure. It was horrible to see the
massive bird hopping along with the little terrier powerless
in her talons; the strongest man in the world could not
prize those talons apart. The dog turned sideways and
struggled to run one way while being dragged the other.

Falconers must be prepared for emergencies. Sam pulled
off his sheepskin jacket and threw it over the blood-lusting
Berkut. The eagle found herself blacked out and held down

while still gripping the dog's loins. Sam threw himself down, pinning the Berkut to the ground. He gripped the feathered leg whose talons were piercing the sad little animal, and the talons opened convulsively to grip the enemy who had come in darkness. The desperate dog bit Sam's wrist before it shot over the wall, howling its fear and pain, escaping down the Parade.

Holding the eagle, Sam yelled, "Quick, Ed, get me a chicken head—anything—"

Ed dropped a chicken head nearby, Sam grabbed his jacket and ran. The furious eagle, on her feet, behaved like a maniac. She pounced on the chicken head, split the skull, and tore at it, which prevented her from associating her experience with her master and his jacket. Once again Sam was given tetanus injections.

Whatever happened, Sam knew he should stick to his training plans, so shortly thereafter Sam, with a bait in his left fist, flew his now sulky and unpredictable eagle the length of the lawn. This is an important exercise which is known to falconers as "calling off."

Sam blew his whistle a couple of times and then made in on the eagle, holding the creance in his right hand so that he could play her a little if she bated away from him and lessen the jar if she suddenly reached the end of the creance. The eagle's attention was fastened on his fully baited left fist; she heaved herself heavily into the air and made in to it.

After a few mouthfuls, Sam replaced his girl on her block, taking the remains of the bait to keep her sharp set. Without a few hunger pangs, the eagle could become lazy

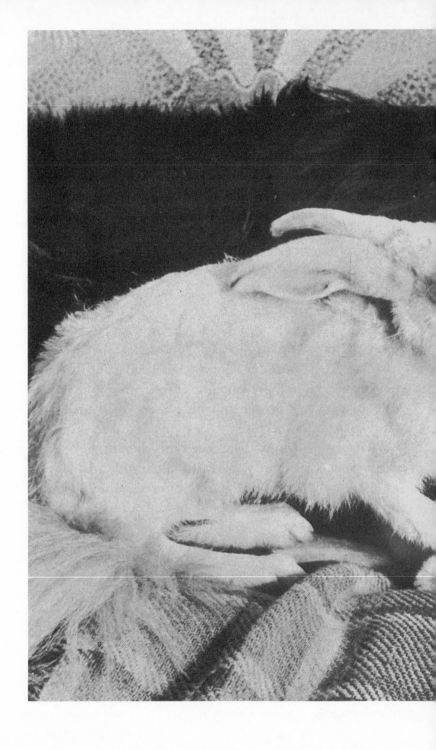

and disobedient. Each day he flew her three times to the fist for tidbits before he set her down for her daily gorge.

One day Sam took her for another ordeal by fire manning walk. The thousandth bate left him exhausted, his arm and shoulder bones ached desperately, but he forced himself to handle her quietly, although inwardly he was controlling his savagery. Finally it was checkmate once more.

But on the way home the eagle behaved better. Sam set her on a branch and called her off upwind a good thirty yards to his fist. Pleased with this, he set her down on a gatepost and made in to her from fifty yards. She came at the second whistle and landed beautifully with a flurry of her splendid wings, taking her reward from his garnished fist. The third flight was from a stump, but her creance tangled and she was brought crashing to the ground in midflight. Sam took her up, and they started for home.

Later that afternoon a sudden heavy shower drenched Atalanta, and he watched as she dried out in the sunshine, preened herself, then perched on her block, dipped her beak into the oily secretion of the gland over her tail, and pulled her long feathers through her beak. Her plumage shone with health.

Quiet days followed, days when the hawk becomes affectionate and playful; days that are the reward of the overstretched falconer, days Sam needed to follow the awful days of the fiery rubbish dump.

Atalanta became so used to the crowds of people who came to see her that she often behaved like an old ham; she amused her audience by bathing, cavorting like some monstrous kitten, tearing up her perches, flying from perch to perch as she picked up sticks and threw them in the air—altogether she enjoyed herself hugely. Sam always found it incongruous to see the royal eagle of the Tartars behaving coyly and being kittenish.

During those happy days Atalanta had a full-blood feed, not the washed meat fed to hunting birds to keep them in trim, until her crop bulged like a cricket ball. She sat rousing her feathers, which indicates a sense of well-being in a healthy bird, cooling her high body temperature. She really appreciated the daily gorge that Sam allowed her, and it was good maintenance; she was a happy bird and the affection between man and bird strengthened.

On a late afternoon Sam stood with one foot on the low wall, his eagle perched happily on his left arm supported by his raised knee. Atalanta turned her head and her cruelly curved beak began preening Sam's hair, as if his blond head belonged to her own chick. The spectators were delighted. Out of this delight came disaster. Turning his head abruptly in answer to a question, Sam's left eye blacked out and blood poured down his face.

He heard a spectator gasp, "She's torn his eye out!"

Sam flew Atalanta hurriedly to her perch and clasped a hand over his eye. Blood seeped through his fingers and ran down his clothes as he staggered indoors. As help came and people attempted to clean the blood from his eye, Sam asked, "Has she torn my eyeball?"

No one knew; but Sam knew that he was blind in that eye. The doctors were phoned, but they were all out, so Sam returned once again to the casualty department of the hospital. The nurse told him to lie down while she swabbed his eye. The result was magical, his sight came back. In his excited relief he leaped up shouting, "I can see! I can see! Bless you nurse, I'm not blind!" and he seized the surprised nurse and kissed her joyfully.

But Sam's left eyelid had been torn off, and this required a complicated operation, for eyelids cannot be stitched. Next day he went back with his bandaged eye and continued training his golden bird.

TEN

*I care not for a man's religion whose dog or cat
are not the better for it.*
—ABRAHAM LINCOLN

SAM knew that Atalanta had not attacked him; the movement of his own head had thrust the eagle's beak into his skin. Falconers should always be on their guard against such accidents.

Fear is a handicap in training any bird of prey. Sam's courage has never been in question—he likes fierce birds. Because of their fierceness and courage, raptors tame and become manned sooner than gentler birds.

Daily handling was essential for the Berkut, and she needed Sam's entire attention day and night. In addition to full training, Sam wanted his eagle *feather perfect*. This meant imping, joining new feathers to some of her primary and tail feathers. Bent feathers had to be straightened, her beak coped, and her talons cleaned and filed. Samples of her mutes were examined for disease. Parasites and mites, tick and feather lice had to be exterminated. These were only some of the health precautions taken by Sam. In addition, the great bird had to learn to sit quietly while she was weighed each day.

Atalanta weighs approximately twenty-six and a half pounds. Because of her great weight (a possible record) the circulation in her feet is very slow and she must constantly exercise. To keep her feet in trim, some of her perches are padded, some blocks; some are sections cut from tree trunks.

In imping, the falconer stores moulted feathers, so that when a living feather is injured he can replace it with a corresponding one from his supply. Eagles' beaks and talons need coping, since they are too hard to cut in the manner employed with falcons and hawks. Sam short-tied Atalanta to the garden fence and used a crosscut file and a smooth file to do the job. This is a delicate operation; care must be taken not to touch the nerve that runs down the beak and can cause bleeding and pain. In spite of the utmost care, the powerful eagle splintered the fence in her struggles.

Certain furniture was required for manning. There are the bells which the falconer attaches to his hawk so he can find it if it strays. Sam's bells are made of a special alloy and come from Pakistan and Germany; they have the right sound to carry over long distances. The falconer can tell a great deal from the bells. There are special sounds when his eagle hops from one perch to another, sounds for a casual or a serious bait, the pell-mell ringing of one bell when she scratches herself, and the mad jangling when the eagle is angry or attacking.

An essential part of a falconer's equipment is his bag, which must be as light as possible to carry all the paraphernalia necessary for a hunting bird in the field. Eagle country is wild and mountainous, so the bag is hung on a swivel and carried on the falconer's right-hand side to free him for climbing, fording rivers, or running over rough country.

Atalanta, in these early months, had to learn to fly to both the fist and the lure. A lure is a dummy bait of rabbit, hare, or meat placed between a dead bird's wings and attached to a line. It may even be a piece of meat tied to leather and flung so that the eagle flies after it and strikes it in midair or pounces on it after an unsuccessful flight.

Eagles are birds of the crags, and they like to perch as high as possible. Her eight-foot post gives Atalanta a clear view over the promenade and the beach; beyond that is the Irish Sea and in another direction rise the lovely mountains of Merionethshire and of Lleyn.

Atalanta's food is a matter of quality, not quantity. The best food for her is her natural prey, a hare eaten hot and fresh. She eats every part of the animal—liver, fur, intestines, and bones. Her diet is kept varied. Different kinds of dead birds are fed to her with crops and entrails intact. The contents of these birds' crops include seeds and herbs, berries and grasses—natural medicines which protect the Berkut from disease. It is avian medicines like these that provide birds with a natural resistance to diseases which strike down captive birds of prey kept in unnatural conditions.

There was sound reason for this coddling. A hunting eagle's condition in the winter hawking season comes from careful feeding, regulated so that it brings her into the natural condition of a wild mountain eagle. A starved eagle is a weak eagle, only a short way from death. Once below a certain level, the eagle will die. Berkuts are mad keen to kill their own food, but if they are physically weakened by starvation they can neither fly at full strength nor can their enfeebled digestions absorb the food when they kill, and they will die anyway. The careful falconer uses scales daily and never allows his bird to get below its best hunting and flying weight. At this weight an eagle is just as keen to take game as is a starved eagle grown crazy from hunger pangs. The well-fed eagle is the trained athlete of its race; it enjoys overcoming its quarry and is able to digest it.

Sam did not want his Berkut to be in hunting condition just then; he wanted her high, or fat, so each day he felt her keel and the two layers of fat forming along her stomach on which she could live for a couple of weeks without any food, providing the breast and stomach were ripe and full.

Sam's meticulous care was not wasted on Atalanta. She became more splendid every day, better manned, tamer, and she acquired a sort of terrible wild beauty that brought many new visitors to gaze at her. Sam was glad, because strangers were an important part of her manning. By then Sam could fly her the length of the lawn with some confidence. Her favorite perch was the high stone post, and he taught her to fly to it directly so that she would recognize it as a home base when she graduated to free flying.

But for all the merit of using the top of the post as a special landmark, it had been molded into a four-sided pyramid and provided precarious balance. Sam lengthened the creance and put a piece of rabbit on the apex, but the Berkut would not fly to it; she was used to flying to Sam's baited fist. The situation looked hopeless, so Sam himself climbed onto the post, stood up, and whistled.

The eagle turned her head, then took off into the almost gale-force wind blowing in from the sea. He braced himself to balance facing the wind, his back and outstretched fist toward the massive bird. With ponderous wingbeats the Berkut took the air, let the wind hit her, and shot up into it, landing as lightly as thistledown on her master's fist.

It looked very spectacular and the audience clapped loudly. "Did you see that?" Sam shouted. "It won't be long now before she's ready for free flight!"

He climbed down and took Atalanta to her block, then returned to the post whistling to the now keen eagle. She took flight immediately, soaring upwind and landing with the same adroit maneuver, to begin tearing at the rabbit bait.

Climbing down hurriedly, Sam put the now excited eagle back on her block, and she at once set herself for flight. Sam climbed the post again, bracing himself against the wind while he blew a blast on his whistle—but the overeager eagle had already taken flight. She was on Sam before he could stretch out his gauntleted fist—on him, but with no place to land. She soared into the wind above his head, pulling her creance to its end, which brought her crashing down on him—an emergency for which he was *not* prepared.

The Berkut hit Sam across the shoulders as she kek-kek-kekked her panic. The creance tangled around his throat, combined with the gale and the madly flapping eagle, hurled him backward off the post. He struck with his back across the wooden fence and rolled off and over the privet hedge onto the lawn, where he lay twisting about in agony.

So Sam took another trip to the hospital's casualty department, the third in little more than a week. By now the doctors and nurses knew all about Atalanta, and Sam came in for a few mild jeers until one doctor told him to forget about eagle training before it left him blind and crippled. In fact he called it "nonsensical stupidity!" The fall displaced a collarbone, damaged Sam's back, and left him stiff and sore from cuts and bruises. Worse still, he knew the accident had been entirely his own fault.

Next day, bandaged and limping, he carried on with his tight training schedule, carrying the Berkut on his sound left arm and flying her from that arm as well.

Now that Atalanta was coming into hunting trim and Sam's goal of seeing her take her own food in a mountain setting was in sight, there were other problems, other needs. There was the inevitable conflict between a wild, free killer and a civilized human community. Atalanta needed hunting companions, a polecat below ground to chase out rabbits, and a tough, resilient, long-suffering dog to flush ground game—a dog that could work with an eagle whose forebears had for centuries been trained to fly at wolves. Was this another impossible dream?

The rabbits were by far the easier problem. Sam had a little assassin of a polecat, Diana, who was in the process of being manned herself. Polecats are rare in Wales, extinct in England, Scotland, and Ireland. Diana was small and very fierce. Sam fed her by hand and manned her so well that he could carry her in his overcoat pocket. In the daytime she lives in a wire cage; in the evening she can be found in Sam's office, where she eats only from his hands.

Sam wanted his Diana to go down rabbit burrows without a line, and to do that she must be tame enough for him to catch her. He muzzled her and fastened on two little bells; unmuzzled, Diana is a deadly assassin and very courageous. She once fought four cornered rats bigger than herself all at the same time. After a terrific battle, she killed them all.

She is a classic huntress. Sam put the tiny, savage creature into his pocket and led her to where he knew there was a colony of young rabbits. There he took Diana from his pocket and put her down. She disappeared into the grass, keeping downwind and emitting no smell. Thanks to a gland secretion of which rabbits and rats are afraid, no buck rabbit squatted when Diana hunted it, as they do when hunted by a ferret. The young rabbits fed on in the lingering sunlight.

Fast as a striking snake, the polecat shot out her head and snapped the spine of a feeding rabbit, all in total silence. She walked away with her prey in her mouth and disappeared into the cover of the thick grass, while the unsuspecting rabbits continued to feed without missing one of their number. Diana's hunting strategy is that of primitive man—the stalk, the unseen kill performed so silently and expertly that the other animals are unaware of it, and then the quiet withdrawal with the prey.

Diana allowed Sam to pick her up, but she held on to her prey. Arrived home, Sam put her into her cage. She dropped the rabbit in a far corner and curled herself up near to the door to guard it. She was hunting well; with any luck the time would come when she would breed, which is difficult in captivity. In a wild state the male conquers the female and drags her to his lair; but in captivity the female is often killed by the male gripping her wrongly as he serves her. Captivity has another breeding hazard; sometimes the female forms a layer of fat and either reabsorbs her young or dies giving birth. At a university in Wales they have tried for fifteen years to breed polecats, even using a Caesarean birth technique without success.

Diana was Sam's first choice to work underground with his eagle. But Diana was a killer; unless she was lined and wore a mouth mawl (muzzle made of cane) before being put down a burrow, no rabbits would escape for Atalanta to hunt. In fact, Sam finally had to find another polecat of a breed less fierce to hunt with Atalanta.

Even more important was a companion hunter above ground. So Sam began his search for a dog he could train, and almost by accident he came across Shep.

No one can say why a wolf-killing eagle should develop a deep bond of affection, share her life, her love, her rages, her moments of dependence, and her incongruous playfulness with a species of animal she has been bred through the centuries to hunt and kill. But then Shep is no more an ordinary dog than Atalanta an ordinary eagle. Sam gave Shep time to mature and their friendship time to develop, before beginning training them to hunt together.

ELEVEN

Buy a pup and your money will buy
Love unflinching that cannot lie.

—RUDYARD KIPLING

SHEP is a Welsh collie of a rare species. Welsh collies are difficult dogs to come by and are bred especially for working cattle as they have strong herding instincts—so strong that they sometimes attempt to herd cars! Their work is difficult and dangerous; one mistake and the farmer has a dead dog, and months of patient training is thrown away. Shep's father kept on herding cattle long after he was old and slow, which cost him his life, for a bull gored him.

When a Cardiganshire collie bitch whelps, her farmer owner keeps only certain pups from each litter. These are not picked for their strength or beauty but for their obedience, their lack of playfulness, and for the sharpness of their herding instinct. The pups who show a natural instinct for play and have their quota of disobedient ways are killed by an ancient barbaric ritual. The farmer ties a thin cord about their small necks and hangs them to die of slow strangulation.

It was from a mountain farmer such as this that Sam eventually got Shep, who was alive more by accident than design. He was a playful pup, the biggest and most disobedient of the litter. The farmer's children were enchanted by his gaiety and charm and spoilt him even more by romping with him.

The pup was doomed. The farmer could not afford a dog who was a passenger, and he was given to the family of Councillor Glyn Roberts by one of the farmer's children.

In the Roberts' home the pup became a problem. He was a clumsy, rambunctious farm dog, and not even housetrained. A few minutes after his arrival, the neighbors heard smashing and shouting and rushed in to find out he had hit the house like a whirlwind, bounding happily from room to room, mowing down children and furniture alike.

This was too much. No one wanted poor loving Don, as the pup was called. Finally Sam was sent for, because in running his hospital he had found many homes for dogs from the Pwllheli compound.

Sam got his first glimpse of Don as a massive black and white shape bounding up the path. Sam saw a shaggy, happy face, tongue out, as if laughing at him, and then the pup hit Sam like a battering ram, placed his muddy paws around Sam's neck, making him stagger back under the weight. Then Don thrust his intelligent head into Sam's pocket, where he found a few stale sweets.

Friend or rival? © *John D. Drysdale*

Sam put his arms round the huge beast and they did a clumsy dance, the pup thumping Sam's shoulder with his fat paws and licking his face with a tongue that was strongly scented by well-chewed pear drops. For both it was love at first sight. But Sam already had two dogs; he could not take another. He promised to do his best to find a good home for him.

By the following weekend, Don managed to do so much damage around the house that Sam was told that if he could not take Don by Sunday night he would have to be destroyed.

So Sam collected the pup and took him home. Once inside the front door he tore the leash from his new master's hand and rushed around, barking furiously, attempting to make friends with everyone. Delightedly he raced into the television room amid sounds of uproar and rushed out again, apparently wearing the television table complete with the TV itself still blaring away on his broad back until the cord pulled out the plug. The audience resented this intrusion, especially when the set fell and went up in a blue flame that seemed to explode in the ceiling.

The dog was really enjoying himself. He bounded upstairs with Sam hot on his trail. Changing his mind, he reversed and dashed hell-for-leather right through Sam's legs, so that Sam came down on the dog's back like a jockey facing his horse's tail.

This was the last straw. Winded, Sam picked himself up, snatched a cricket bat out of the hall stand, and followed the sounds of the rampage. By now a phonograph had bitten the dust, it kept on revolving slowly as it repeated the

words "Old Shep . . . Old Shep . . ." from the still circling record.

The pup, drunk with success, sprayed the table leg—just
as Sam brought the cricket bat into play. Don gave a howl
of surprised anguish as Sam chased the poor pup out into
the back garden. He returned to the house, bruised and
sore, and picked up the phonograph which was still grind-
ing wearily, "Old Shep . . . Old Shep . . ."

"I'm changing Don's name to Shep," Sam told his audience grimly. "The stinker. I like him and I'm going to train
him. He's full of affection and baby play, even if he is too
big and too old for such a carry-on, but he's intelligent and
in two weeks you won't know him."

For the next ten days Shep suffered an iron discipline
and it paid off. The cricket bat was discarded and never
used again; an inflection in his master's voice hurt Shep
more than any blow. In two weeks Shep was house-trained,
he walked at heel, went out by himself for the paper, carried the shopping basket, sat up, shook hands, was civilized.

Sam's new dog was super-intelligent and he worshiped
his master, his eyes followed him everywhere. When he was
out of doors Shep was still clumsy; he would walk into
things such as lampposts because he wandered along gazing
back at Sam. He was full of affection and playfulness and allowed children to drag him about; he was, in embryo, the
best dog that Sam had ever owned.

Shep and Atalanta were soon introduced. If Atalanta's
fierce eyes bored into Shep, then Shep's brown eyes that
looked so lovingly at his master were kept warily on the
eagle. Both eagle and dog were jealous of their master, and

Finding lost Atalanta was Shep's triumph

Shep knew that the eagle had his measure. They tangled a few times, but the intelligent dog realized that the curved beak, the cruel talons, plus her uncertain temper made Atalanta too formidable for him. Many times she tried to take a chunk out of the dog, but Shep's herding instinct enabled him to take successful evading action. A long period passed while the eagle and the dog learned to be friends.

Sam kept many small and rare animals and birds, and from time to time these were raided by predators. One night the cats wiped out a little colony of rock doves which Sam hoped to breed and establish once again on the cliffs of Wales. The cats, besides being killers, were expert thieves and stole the animals' foods. Sam got an idea for eliminating the dangerous, bloodthirsty pests. He baited his lawns with meat in the evenings and left Atalanta out all night, tethered by her long creance. The experiment worked. Every morning Sam would gather up partly eaten carcasses of cats and bury them at once.

One morning he was horrified to find not only two dead cats but a mangy white and fawn mongrel as well. Another morning, and a dead black-haired mongrel. This upset Sam. He could not expect Atalanta to differentiate between wild cats and domesticated animals whose owners left them out all night, so he stopped baiting the lawns. He did not feel that he had committed any crime; both dogs and cats were trespassers. As usual the animals suffered for the owners' carelessness. He took Atalanta up to his bedroom again at night, feeling that someone might try to injure his bird in reprisal.

By now Atalanta gave flying exhibitions every day over a

measured mile, leaving behind Sam's racing pigeons. He timed her flying against the wind from Llanbedrog Headland to her own lawn post, a distance of four and a half miles; she made these flights in three and a half minutes. Flying free she would spiral up into the sky, soaring and gliding lazily in the thermals she found by instinct. Atalanta's habits were those of the golden eagle clan, and golden eagles are hunting eagles; they swoop on their flying prey in a closed-wing dive at the end of which they snatch their prey upward, as opposed to falcons which strike their prey down. When she heard Sam's thunder whistle she would come in, a glorious sight, swooping to land lightly as a feather on her master's fist. The eagle was as gentle as a kitten with people and children; toddlers stroked her shining plumage. But a fierce light blazed in her eyes when she saw a furry animal, which represented a delicious meal just waiting for her strike.

This was a splendid time for Atalanta, but Sam knew it couldn't last forever. Three incidents in particular convinced him of this. One morning a lovely little white poodle was standing on the Parade wall when Atalanta swooped down in play. Without interrupting the pattern of her flight along the seafront, she swept him up in one set of talons. There was nothing Sam could do except whistle Atalanta to his fist.

The bird ignored him and flew down to shelter still clutching the poodle. By some miracle the little dog was unhurt; it actually seemed to be playing with the great eagle when Sam snatched it up, not really believing his eyes, and returned it to its outraged owners. Thinking about it later, the only explanation he could find was that he had filed Atalanta's hooked beak and her talons; and if she had taken the poodle out of playfulness and not hunger, she had not squeezed it hard enough to hurt it.

The next crisis came when a friendly Welsh terrier called Tess, which had been left in Sam's care by its owners while they were on holiday, followed him out onto Atalanta's lawn. This time the Berkut, certainly in play, grabbed Tess's hindquarters and dragged the struggling, protesting little dog toward' her shelter. In a few seconds Tess was freed and no harm done.

But the third incident was much more serious. A local troublemaker used to pass Atalanta's lawn on his way to the sand dunes where he took his greyhound to hunt rabbits. He kept his greyhound hungry and had made it vicious. Each time it went by Atalanta, it barked and leaped at her. The angry eagle was tethered, so the dog was fairly safe. Sam warned the owner to walk his greyhound on the other side of the road, to no avail.

One day Sam was flying Atalanta from the sand dunes, and she zoomed home to her high post. Unluckily the young man and his greyhound were passing. As usual the dog jumped up at the eagle. Atalanta simply dropped onto the snarling greyhound, her iron talons raked its back until it howled with pain. It tried to get away but the eagle's grip tightened through its back. The dog lurched to the center of the roadway, but the old instinct of the wolf killer made the eagle plunge her other talons through its skull. When Sam arrived, the stupid owner was still yelling to his dog:

"Git 'er Bob—git 'er!"

Common sense told Sam that Atalanta would have to cease her seafront flights. It was a serious problem. Such a tremendous bird needed daily exercise at that time of year. During a moult, an eagle develops an extra blood supply for its new feathers so it is not quite as necessary for her to have long exercising flights. But Atalanta's moult was over.

Flying her away from the local seafront was much too dangerous because of such man-made obstacles as telegraph wires, fences, and other things. One possibility was to fly her in the nearby mountains, but strong winds and bad weather made this impossible for many days of the year; still, Sam felt he must try it.

Seven miles from Pwllheli, Nefyn Mountain rises up, and a car can be driven almost to the top. It is treeless and so an ideal place from which to fly an eagle. Sam, with his binoculars, could follow her flight for miles in any direction.

A summer sunset from the top of Nefyn is a superb sight. In the distance rise the ranges of Snowdonia and Merionethshire. Near at hand are the tree-covered mountains of Garn Fadryn, Garn Madryn, and Garn Boduan. Below lie the cliffside golf course of Morfa Nefyn and the coastline with its bird cliffs such as Carreg-y-Llam, where thousands of seabirds breed; then on across the bay is the Isle of Anglesea.

Sam decided to release Atalanta from the top of Nefyn, but once there he became very nervous. A mistaken decision might lose him his eagle. He steeled himself and took her onto his fist and flew her into the northwest wind blowing strongly from the sea. It was a glorious sight to see the royal eagle flying free in a natural habitat; to her master she seemed the ultimate beauty of creation.

The sun dropped like a ball of fire behind the far mountains. Sam and his companion Ron Semmens stood on the top of Nefyn for more than three hours, binoculars to their eyes, following Atalanta's every movement as she reconnoitered her surroundings with minute care. Three times she returned nearby but ignored Sam's frantic shouts and whistles. She planed about with complete independence, quartering the ground, then lazily spiraled up to her pitch and floated off on a further reconnaisance of a distant mountain or a bird-rock.

Dusk began to fall. Ron saw Atalanta herding and chasing a flock of sheep down the side of the next mountain, playing as eagles do. In a little while she landed on a boulder and went on calmly watching the sheep grazing contentedly around her.

"Will she take sheep, Sam?" Ron asked.

"Of course not, the wool's too thick. She could take a lamb in season, but it's unlikely she would. It worries me because farmers don't know she won't, and one of them might take a shot at her."

Atalanta, taking flight, interrupted them. It was a wonderful sight as she fell into the wind, threw up and turned to soar lazily out of sight toward Trevor Mountain in the fast-gathering dusk. For Sam it was the beginning of three days of tension and despair.

TWELVE

Thou art beautiful, O my love . . . terrible
as an army with banners.
—SONG OF SONGS

THAT night Sam could not sleep. Before daybreak he was
back on the top of Nefyn. With him was a lure of stuffed
hare with red meat attached to it, and as the light increased
he stood swinging the lure round his head and giving piercing blasts on his whistle. When a hawk is lost, the experienced falconer returns to the spot from which it was originally flown and stands swinging the lure for hour after
hour, if necessary for day after day, because hawks so often
return to the place from which they have been flown.

That afternoon Sam was rewarded by his first glimpse of
the wandering Atalanta. Over the bird-rock of Carreg-y-
Llam he saw a cloud of birds black against the sky. They
seemed to be drifting lazily after a black glider, Atalanta.

"Thank goodness she's still around," Sam told himself. She disappeared and the birds gradually dispersed. Sam felt heavily despondent as he stood there, swinging the lure, swinging . . . swinging . . . until his arm ached and darkness fell on the world and on his spirit.

Next day he took Shep with him to the mountaintop. It was tough walking for a man—walls, barbed-wire fences, and rocks, underfoot gorse and bracken, ferns, and all the upland vegetation was knee-high, prickly at best, often cruelly spiky and almost impenetrable. But this was Shep's heritage, the kind of terrain for which he was bred, and he took all these obstacles in his stride, pleasing Sam with the ease with which he surmounted the difficulties.

All day Sam swung the lure, and his heart became heavier as evening approached without a sign of his beloved eagle. Atalanta was already so much a part of his life. He sat down forlorn and discouraged and took out his brandy flask. He patted Shep; the big dog was not discouraged, wagging his white-tipped tail as he curled it across his back in an arc. Sam looked at him curiously. He was still less than a novice at hunting with Atalanta, and Sam did not know all his ways as intimately as he knew Atalanta's.

"What is it, boy? You've been excited for a long time. D'you want to go home?"

Clearly puzzled, Sam threw down the leather gauntlet and ordered Shep to pick it up. "Go find her boy. Shep boy, find her."

Shep, the gauntlet held in his jaws, bounded away down the mountain. Sam muttered, "Bloomin' idiot of a dog," but did not call him back. He stood up and began to swing the lure again.

Half an hour later Sam saw Shep. He was sitting on a high knoll about a mile away, still holding the gauntlet in his mouth. Then a strange thing happened. Two ravens suddenly changed course and flew down the knoll and began to dive-bomb something apparently near where Shep was sitting.

Unless a falconer can read natural signs, he cannot find a quarry for his hawk; he has to know the behavior patterns of both birds and beasts. Sam knew what the ravens were diving at. All birds of prey are mobbed by other birds. He was on his way through the cruel undergrowth immediately.

Sam went as rapidly as he could up the steep side of the knoll. What he saw when he reached the top drove the weariness from his sagging body and filled his eyes with tears of relief. Facing Shep was Atalanta. Fierce-eyed and with raised hackles, eagle and dog weighed each other up.

It was only a matter of seconds before his hawk was on Sam's fist and they started for home. Atalanta had had three days of freedom, but Sam, too, had learned his own lessons through those days of bitter unhappiness and loss. Atalanta's reclamation was Shep's triumph, and Sam now knew that they were both ripe for the development Sam planned for them, a hunting partnership. While all falconers train dogs to work with their hawks, eagles are a law unto themselves. Shep's own herding instincts had sent him after Atalanta, but he had much to learn before the eagle would understand that he was her hunting companion and a member of her family. From now on they would live, sleep, and stay together at all times.

That night Shep slept in Sam's bedroom at the foot of

Atalanta's screen perch. Next morning the great bird had her talons bound with adhesive plaster; over this Sam put a leather glove and lined the fingers with cotton wool. He filed the death-dealing beak to a greater bluntness. He knew that Atalanta must learn respect for Shep; it would be Shep's job to tackle her and worry (mock attack) her up into the air, all the while avoiding injury, perhaps death, from her deadly talons.

All that morning Sam encouraged Shep to keep the eagle on the move. Brave, shaggy Shep charged her when she flew, her great wings shadowing him, or when she tried to use her raking talons from the springboard of her outspread tail. Shep took avoiding action and barked all the time as he circled her, then came at her, shoulder first, head down. In out . . . in out . . . the dog soon mastered the grounded eagle's clumsy rushes. Sam encouraged Shep to keep it up so that the harassed eagle found peace only by flying to a window ledge. Then he called Shep away from her. He chose the window ledge as the place onto which Shep must always herd her in his absence or if she behaved badly.

This long, tense morning began the real companionship between eagle and dog, and it founded a unique relationship that has lasted for years. By the end of the week Atalanta was again giving her seafront flying exhibitions, only now Shep ran along the Parade on patrol, up and down, as the eagle flew overhead.

Sam was no longer worried that Atalanta would attack stray dogs. Shep was on duty, he would not let her get into mischief. In time the dog became almost as well known as Atalanta herself.

Free-flying exercise on the shore

Weeks were spent flying Atalanta, aided by Shep, at every variety of game Sam could find. The diversity of her education is reflected in Sam's diary:

"Flew Atalanta free on Nefyn Mountain. She soared and glided for two hours. Killed two hares. I had to walk three miles over rough country to reclaim her after the second hare. Dusk was falling, I would not risk having Shep chase her when she might rake-off into darkness.

"Atalanta still had food in her crop, and she had not cast and so could not be flown at game. Racing against rock doves and racing pigeons in exercise flights over a measured mile, she won all seven races although the pigeons were thrown before Atalanta left the fist. Mostly the eagle won by the length of the Parade. Rain today, and gales, confining Atalanta to seafront flights.

"From Llanbedrog Headland Atalanta killed two gulls, a jackdaw, and three rabbits. She was mobbed by birds, which were safe as long as they flew above her. She stooped on those flying beneath her, gulls and a jackdaw, snatched them out of the air, crushing them in her talons and letting them fall like squeezed fruit; she had no further interest in them.

"Atalanta cast too late to go to the mountains. She flew from Llanbedrog Headland, four and a half miles to her landing post, against a red homing pigeon. Three minutes and thirty-five seconds it took her; the pigeon was so far behind that it was not timed. For two days weather conditions for flying at game have been impossible.

"Had a hard day's walking round Rival Mountains. Put up two foxes, one went to cover in a badger's set. The eagle killed the other in a stoop and we heard the thundering rush of it far along the mountain side. After the kill Atalanta's left wing drooped. I took her up, we went home and put her in her mews under the sunray lamp.

"Christmas Day. Accepted an invitation for hare-hawking on Anglesea. It is flat, open country. My eagle killed five hares in seven flights. Flew the eagle at a beautiful white snow goose. She could have taken it but did not, she only harassed it. We were glad she only wanted to play instead of binding to the lovely bird. Atalanta's wing is quite cured.

"Flew Atalanta at pheasants. For some reason she raked away from cock pheasants; perhaps because of their exotic plumage, she refused to fly them. I brought home a dead cock pheasant. Each time it was offered to Atalanta she bated away from it, yet when I cut it up she ate it with relish.

"Invited to a farm where a fox is killing poultry. The farmer cleared the fields near the woods of sheep. Beaters chased the fox into the open. Atalanta could not kill it skulking along the sheep walls, then it ran across the farm-yard. The eagle killed a mangy farm dog which went mad when it saw her, barking and running to attack. Shep was held by being attacked by three other dogs. The farmer called the dead dog a bloody nuisance and said his dogs fended for themselves, he did not bother to feed them.

"It is a peculiar day, the wind continually changes direction. Took Shep and Atalanta to Nefyn; Ron Semmens and his wife came too. Atalanta was set upon by two peregrines and we saw a fascinating flying display. Atalanta bated off

Hunting on a hillside of Atalanta's adopted country
© *John D. Drysdale*

my fist and made off along a gully, zigzagging as the wind hit her from different directions, she could not get an up-draft until she reached the end of the gully. Then she threw up like a winged rocket, hurtled down again, and leveled off a few feet above the mountainside. She followed the contour of the mountain downward at breakneck speed. Above her flew a long-winged peregrine, hurtling itself at the eagle. The Berkut's object was to fly close to the ground and to let the peregrine crash into the mountainside. The peregrine was too clever for this; it pulled out of its stoop to throw up into the sky again at a terrific speed, like a fighter plane strafing a passenger aircraft. For a few seconds both birds disappeared around the mountain; when they reappeared there were two peregrines. One of them tried to fly beneath the Berkut to keep her high in the air while its mate positioned itself for the famous peregrine stoop, one of the most thrilling sights in nature. This elegant killer is the best bird of prey for killing in the air. Frederick II of Hohenstaufen, the thirteenth-century authority on hawking, called the peregrine "the truly noble falcon." At the end of its terrific two-hundred-mile-an-hour stoop, with its scythe-like wings folded and the wind shrilling through its flattened pinions, it takes its prey from above and kills instantly by the terrific midair collision or stuns its victim and administers the *coup de grâce* on the ground with its toothed beak.

"My friends and I had seen a splendid example of how basically the flight of a falcon differs from the flight of a hawk. Falcons fly high and wait-on; hawks fly low over the ground and in direct pursuit of their quarry; and both species adapt their flights and use their intelligences to meet each different hunting demand."

Sam speaks of the Berkut as being in her element that day and how for two hours the three friends watched the aerial acrobatics. This was a more exciting spectacle than flying the mighty Berkut at game, for now the twenty-six-odd-pound eagle with her nine-foot-plus wingspan was proving herself equal in flying ability to the aerial maneuvering of the world's greatest flyers, buccaneers of the sky, each weighing about two pounds.

At last Atalanta landed on a sheep wall near her master. She was open beaked and panting. As Sam and his friends drove down the mountainside with Atalanta, the two peregrines hovered high above them in the way of wind-hovering kestrel hawks, motionless against the keen atmosphere of the sky.

THIRTEEN

Here's to them that shoot and miss. —THE FALCONERS' TOAST

AFTER their return that evening, Atalanta made mainly training flights. Now Shep, keyed up and anxious to please Sam, became harder to train than Atalanta. Then a letter came from Eddie Hallam of Ribor Castle, Matlock, of the British Fauna Trust, telling how foxes had killed most of a rare species of duck the trust wanted to conserve. Trapping and shooting had failed; Hallam asked if it would be possible to fly Atalanta over the peaks, and if so would she find and kill the foxes?

Before he could give a definite answer, Sam had to give Atalanta special tests. He flew her among cattle and horses to see whether the animals of the Fauna Trust would divert her and if hides would attract her as did soft-furred animals such as rabbits, hares, and foxes.

Setting her on a gatepost, Sam sent Shep to her. She flew a hundred yards to his whistle, first zigzagging over the cattle. In her last exercise flight she zoomed onto his fist, begging rather touchingly for the reward of an almost fleshless chicken wing. She had passed her test.

That afternoon he arranged with three friends to go with him to Ribor Castle. If Atalanta was to stretch her intelligence as well as her wings, she must fly against as many big game birds as possible and against foxes.

On New Year's Eve Sam and Atalanta left the dejected Shep and drove away in the estate car, taking along a stand perch for Atalanta. That first night in Cheshire it was bitterly cold, with ice, frost, and snow; but this only delighted the great Berkut, warm beneath the cape of her alula wings. She slept peacefully, white with snow, her head tucked under the shoulder of one wing, her bastard wings across her shoulders, one foot kept warm in her feathered breast, and the perching foot covered by an apron of feathers.

Next day Sam expected to fly Atalanta at Ribor late in the afternoon, but an exercise flight on the way developed into a marathon soaring and gliding exhibition from which she refused to return for two hours.

By the time they arrived at Ribor it was dusk. Eddie Hallam, who ran the sanctuary, was eager to get Atalanta into the air to hunt the marauding foxes before it became really dark. He himself owned three golden eagles, but none had been trained to fly free and none was a quarter as heavy as Atalanta.

In the teeth of the bitter nor'easter scything around the castle with its eerie keening, Atalanta was taken out on Sam's fist and faced into the gale-force wind. The highest vantage point for miles around was in front of the castle and, with its up-currents and thermals and no danger from fences or telegraph wires, it provided ideal flying for Atalanta.

The little group of men looking into the snowbound wilderness below could see no animals of any kind. But Atalanta's fierce eyes, beneath their overhanging brows, not only have much greater power than the human eye but can see all around the retina, unlike the human eye which sees only in funnels. Moreover, any kind of movement flares up in the eagle's eye.

For a time the statuesque eagle tracked the other birds flying across the sky. She balanced on taut, outstretched wings. Dusk drew in fast, but there were bright patches in the sky. Suddenly the Berkut tensed, her talons gripped the gauntlet, and Sam thought, "Hang it all, I'll let her have a go!"

He threw her into the wind, easing his aching arms and relieving the painful pressure of her talons. Immediately the Berkut showed her tremendous powers of flight. She beat heavily low down and sideways to the wind before facing into it. She threw up at terrific speed, planing away in an effortless glide which carried her two or three miles without a single wingbeat. Everyone knew that the eagle had sighted something, but whatever it was, it went to ground and she lost it.

Atalanta's long glide into the distance was a tactical maneuver. The golden eagle's head has such mobility that it can be turned in a complete circle, dislocating and somehow reforming the vertebrae of the neck at will—something no naturalist or scientist has been able to explain. With this circular sweep of the neck, Atalanta had complete sight-command of any movement on the ground or higher than her own flight.

Whatever it was that she had seen and then lost had left its cover again. The eagle banked around in the wind and with no special finesse began a stooping dive. This carried her with the wind screaming through her pinions, so that the wing tips curled upward as she zoomed toward a fox that had broken cover at remarkable speed and was making for a coppice of birch trees. The fox had made a fatal mistake. The eagle cut the distance between herself and the fox easily and hit the fox in the neck with one set of outstretched talons and with the other set gripped its mask, hurling it over. A dog-fox's muzzle is thicker than a vixen's, so the poor brute gave an awful scream before Atalanta mantled him and drove her talons again and again through his skull with her convulsive clutches. With sheer brute strength and the lust of the kill, she dragged the dead fox around, and when the men reached her there, she crouched, tearing beaksful of fur from under its body, the wind catching the fur tufts in its gusts and blowing them away like a flight of red butterflies.

Sam's gauntlet was baited with red meat; he took her up and she devoured it ravenously. One of the men put the fox, unnoticed by her, into a sack. When her prey had disappeared she yelped, and the men thought she was begging for more food and laughed at her. But Sam knew that some chain reaction had affected her wild mechanism; this was her way of pleading to be released so that she could investigate her kill. But it was semitwilight, they were in strange country, and Sam thought it best not to fly her again that evening.

This decision did not suit Atalanta. She struggled wildly and her talons tore a gash in Sam's uncovered hand. The pain was so great that for a moment he released his hold on her jesses. With a tumbling half roll the eagle fell to the ground, got to her feet, and ran with outstretched wings, flapping and sending the snow showering about her as her wings hit the ground. Then the great bird rose heavily in the air.

Sam's two falconer friends were puzzled because the eagle rose only about fifty feet to fly across the snow-covered grass ridge before she landed again, beating on the snow with her wings and voicing her displeasure. They thought this amazing eagle behavior.

Then, suddenly, they saw the cause of it all. A hillock of crisp snow opened up and a vixen bounded out, fleeing pell-mell down the mountain with her magnificent brush trailing straight out behind her. She had burrowed into the snow for cover and had been lying perdu in the fox's wily way.

Atalanta circled low over her prey, but the fox sniffed the wind as she ran and turned at a tangent, crosswind, among a patch of bramble and bracken so that the eagle could not get in her strike. They were all amazed that the vixen had avoided the eagle because of the fierce up-currents that lifted the huge bird with them. She gathered speed before banking round in a terrific half roll to hurl herself at the

Flying against foxes stretches intelligence as well as wings © *S. Barnes*

running fox which had reached the quarry's edge and was moving among the boulders along the lip of the precipice.

Atalanta matched the vixen's cunning. She dive-bombed her until she ran into a U-shaped culvert; then the eagle landed on her splayed tail, backpedaled her wings, and yelped loudly, the sound echoing around the hillside. The fox ran panic-stricken in circles, driven by the grounded eagle. The circles grew smaller as the vixen was pushed nearer the quarry's edge. In desperation the terrified vixen gave the fox's maniacal laugh of fear as she sank low on her haunches, then sprang with a twisting jump to attack Atalanta with slashing jaws and needle-sharp teeth.

The eagle threw herself backward and her legs shot out in an adroit movement which nearly stopped the vixen in midair. Only one set of talons caught the animal's haunches. It was not the best grip, but it was powerful enough to hurl her over. With a muscular twist, the vixen tore herself free; in her terror and pain she leaped into space, her screams echoing back from the quarry's edge.

When the falconers arrived the Berkut stood panting and breathless, apparently bewildered by the disappearance of her prey. The light was fading. Sam peered below and saw the rufous body of the fox twisted grotesquely over the boulders, a fallen red banner. Atalanta was the heroine of that encounter, and Sam gave her the full crop of meat she craved. Even those terrible eyes were luminous with life now that the death light had faded, and the wind that powered her destruction became soothing through her loosened breast feathers. The killer-foxes destroyed, she rested, her body one with her world.

FOURTEEN

The partridge dreamed not of the falcon's foot.
—THOMAS SACKVILLE, LORD BUCKHURST

IN the early morning Pwllheli Parade is deserted except for
the milkman on his morning rounds. Sam thought it would
be good exercise for them both if he threw Atalanta up
from the wall to give her height enough to sweep out over
the beach and fly back to her own perch. This meant heavy
flying for her, broken only by gliding.

In the deserted surroundings the eagle looked colossal as
she flew with slow, strong wingbeats over the sand and
toward the sea, taking advantage of the faint breeze stirred
up by the swell. Atalanta needs thermals or winds to remain
airborne, and when she could find neither she banked
around and flew laboriously toward home. The going was
heavy and the eagle lazy; she planed to the end of the wall

and then, instead of zooming out over the road to her garden perch, she decided to land on a large square block of concrete marking the end of the wall. There she waited, panting and motionless, for Sam to come and take her up.

It was simply bad luck that a local crank should come by. He had always had some sort of phobia about Atalanta— he would bang a tin with his heavy walking stick whenever he came near her. He was known locally for such crazy antics; most people gave him a wide berth.

When he saw Atalanta land on the wall, he picked up a piece of bread from a pile of food that had been left there for the gulls and dropped it beside her. The eagle cocked her head inquiringly, and she was eyeing the bread with interest when he raised his heavy walking stick and struck her a crashing blow on the side of the head. It toppled her over. He swung his stick again and swept her off the concrete wall onto the sand of the beach below.

Atalanta, who had never known unkindness from a human, did not understand what had happened. She was injured and dazed, and she flapped round and round in abortive efforts to get airborne. The man jumped onto the sand and picked up a big stone and tried to smash it down on the half-stunned eagle. Luckily he missed. Atalanta, flapping her massive wings, stumbled along into the sand dunes with the man running after her.

Sam had been able to see it all from a distance. Running along the Parade and shouting to the milkman to hold deliveries and to watch everything, he got to within two hundred yards of the end of the wall and called to Atalanta, shouting, "Come on, girl . . . come on. . . ."

By this time Atalanta had managed to get on top of the ridge of a sand dune, a possible take-off point. She faced into the faint breeze and made despairing efforts to get airborne. Again and again the Berkut's heavy wings crashed into the thick star grass of the dunes, then the great body began to lift. She rose about six feet and flew heavily, trying to get to Sam, who ran toward her as fast as he could. She circled him and landed on the nearby wall.

The attacker was also running down the Parade, waving his stick, swearing he was going to kill the eagle before Sam's eyes. Sam stood between Atalanta and the man who, when he reached Sam, lashed out at his head with his heavy walking stick. The blow landed instead on the thickly padded shoulder of Sam's sheepskin jacket. Fortunately Sam is a boxer, so he stood his ground, and as the man rushed to attack, he ran into Sam's fist, which tore a gash above his eye. But the man was tough and came back at Sam. They are both big, tall men, and for a couple of minutes it was all Sam could do to hold him off. Finally, both men fell heavily on the asphalt prom, Sam luckily on top. Blood flew everywhere; the man struggled feebly, then lay unconscious. By this time the milkman had arrived.

"Is he dead, Sammy?" he said in an awed voice. "He's in a hell of a mess!"

"Come on, we'd better help the poor devil. Sit him up. I didn't attack him, I only tried to hold him off. His face hit the ground when he fell."

The milkman agreed. "Yes, I saw."

Luckily for Sam, others had seen the incident. He and the milkman struggled to pick up the injured man who was, by then, coming to. He was a heavy man and he swore and spat blood at them both. The milkman went back to his round, and Sam went for help and advice from a retired police superintendent living nearby. There he learned his opponent had attacked the superintendent, whose first reaction to Sam's story was to say he wished Sam had killed him!

When Sam returned to the Parade the man had gone; but the next two weeks three different hospitals put seventeen stitches in his face. This roused the local police who made inquiries and took statements from Sam and the milkman. It was a nasty experience, worst of all for Atalanta.

Unlike a dog, a bird of prey cannot be punished and then show obedience. Sam tried to take his eagle hunting, but she merely flew out of sight and caused a wearying search over hill, cliff, and mountain, from Nefyn, Carreg-y-Llam, through the Trevor and Rival mountains.

On the third day Sam was motoring along the hill road between Nefyn and Llithfaen when, by an amazing piece of luck, he saw his eagle's silhouette on a rock jutting from a bare hillside. Slowly and with difficulty he climbed the hill to approach Atalanta downwind—if she took off, it would have to be upwind toward him.

Sam could see that one man's cruel treachery had already cost her some of her tameness and trust. This was heartbreaking for Sam, who could see as he climbed that she was already tensed for take-off.

He slipped on the loose shale and Atalanta fell into the wind and was away in a long, low glide along the contour of the hillside. As she approached him on his right side, Sam leaped at her like a goalkeeper diving for the ball. By some miracle, his hand gripped the finger feathers at the tip of her right wing and brought her down. She toppled over and Sam pounced onto her. The struggle lasted only for a few seconds of blinding wing blows and the fierce tearing of beak and talons; that was long enough for those steely talons to badly lacerate Sam's hands. But he managed to keep his hold: scarred hands were a small price to pay for his beautiful Berkut.

Once more they returned to her lawn; her training had to begin all over again, almost from scratch. Once more her screen perch was installed in Sam's bedroom. She bated wildly if anyone went near her, which was hardly surprising. Manning began over again; at all costs those bonds of affection so painstakingly forged among the man, the eagle, and the dog must be reestablished, and as quickly as possible.

Reclaiming Atalanta proved to be a long haul, one which would have been impossible if the eagle's nervous system had been disrupted by the beating.

Fortunately nature was on Atalanta's side by causing her moult to begin. This meant that she had greatly reduced powers of flight. Her hackle feathers on head and neck and her wing-covert feathers became washed out. As the hackle feathers became a weak buff color, they were replaced by new feathers that soon regained their glorious red-gold tinge (the reason Atalanta and her subspecies are called golden eagles). She needed extra food to make an additional blood supply for her new feathers, so flying exercise was not quite as necessary.

By May she was eating well and getting fat. There is an old saying, "A fat hawk maketh a lean horse and a weary falconer." But his portly eagle did not weary Sam; at last he could give her the untethered freedom of her lawn and she was happy, occasionally going off by herself to fly along the beach. Sam never allowed her to become bored; she even tried nest making—in her wild state she would have spent this time brooding on her nest while her mate flew and hunted for her—but like most female eagles she was very bad at it. She became very jealous if Sam played too long with Shep or, if he stood talking to some strangers longer than she thought he should, Atalanta would drive them away, stabbing at them with her talons.

At times of her own choosing, Atalanta becomes flirtatious with Sam, and then it is hard to remember her as a deadly projectile that drops from the sky or the demon that has scarred her master so terribly. She becomes entirely feminine; her quirky humor seems conscious of the fun her comic waddle brings or the coyly provoking rouse when, feathers on end, head sunk between the heavy curves of her wings, her fierce eyes closed to contented slits, she transforms herself into a shapeless copper gnome.

When it is cold, Atalanta does a comic turn trying to bathe; her talons slip and make skatelike cuts on the frozen water. She loses her temper, tears up the lawn, and acts like a spoiled child, which makes Sam laugh, at the same time worrying him because he must keep a careful watch lest she become a pet, for this must not happen.

Sam's mother, a tiny old lady of eighty-two, is about the only person who refuses to put up with any nonsense from

Atalanta was becoming more splendid every day

Atalanta. If she thinks Atalanta is giving her any cheek when she comes to the gate, she bumps the great eagle with her shopping bag, which makes Atalanta give a very undignified jump onto the opposite gatepost. If Atalanta decides to cross the road, the old lady, suspecting that Atalanta is nothing but a gossip that must see what the neighbors are doing, follows her across the street carrying her folded newspaper and chases her home again. But the eagle is incurably curious, she likes to see what is going on, so when the old lady goes indoors she waddles back across the road, usually without much success, for Sam sends Shep after her and she flies back clucking her displeasure.

One dawn Atalanta disappeared in a gale-force wind and did not return for her evening meal. Sam began to worry about her and, when the telephone rang early the next morning, he answered with a terrible sinking of heart. It was from a man in Leicestershire; he sounded worried.

"I have five hundred pigeons and your eagle keeps landing on my pigeon loft. Will you come and get her—or tell me what to do?"

Sam was so relieved that he began to laugh, "You're hundreds of miles from me. I'll tell you what to do. Get a dustbin lid and bang it like hell!"

An hour or so before dusk the errant Atalanta arrived home. She ate a hearty meal, then bathed and preened herself before her usual admiring audience.

Why are there always some people who cannot bear to see an animal—or a man for that matter—going peacefully about their lawful pursuits? Atalanta went her wild and wonderful way, unaware that she had become the object of a hate campaign; early in November the Pwllheli Council sent Sam a Nuisance Abatement Notice, Public Health Act, 1936, the gist of which was that his eagle was a nuisance and "prejudicial to the health of the adjoining residents."

Deciding not to be annoyed by this document, Sam sent the town clerk, who was, incidentally, a friend, a pleasant letter pointing out that Atalanta is under control at all times; during her free flights Shep follows her and does not permit her to land except on her home lawns. The sole exceptions are when crowds of people want to photograph her and prevent her from landing on her own block. Even then she lands as close to her lawn as possible, and the crowd opens for her and she waddles along home with Shep in attendance. Sam suggested that the Councillors should come and see the bird for themselves.

As for the question of health, Atalanta bathes before every feed, her block is scalded after she eats, her lawn is never soiled. Ticks, feather lice, and mites would be fatal to her. She is watched over far more carefully than most babies.

As a result of this letter, the order was held over pending the occurrence of an actual incident witnessed by five people. The courts are Welsh, Sam Barnes is English, and as his incensed solicitor told him, "The Archangel Gabriel could not win a case for Sam Barnes in that court!" But Sam would not accept that; he appealed.

The local Council was savaged by animal lovers. Sam asked for a hearing from the Pwllheli Council. The Council's officers could find no cause for complaint, nor could one

. . . better manned, tamer

... acquiring a terrible wild beauty that brought visitors to gaze at her

single complainant be found, save for one unidentified source, clearly not local, who claimed that one day the giant eagle would swoop down on a child and kill it! This was nonsense, but how was Sam to prove it so when his letters to the Council went unopened, he was not allowed a hearing, and the source remained anonymous?

Atalanta's friends were indignant. A deputation of local children, hearing newspaper reports of complaints about Atalanta discussed by their parents, came to Sam's door and handed him a grubby piece of paper. It was a "Save Atalanta" petition carrying more than six hundred signatures.

"Please leave Mr. Barnes and his Eagle alone. Atalanta harms no one, we all love to watch her, and to pat her."

Like a tall Pied Piper, Sam led the children to Alderman Richard Williams, J.P., who was also touched by the youngsters' anxiety and released the petition to the press.

So much public sympathy was aroused by the children's devotion that the Councillors changed their views, some even coming to Atalanta's defense.

The abatement order was still in force. Sam was utterly sick of the silly fuss and tried to forget it, flying his eagle every day. It was wonderful to see flocks of small birds surrounding Atalanta on her lawn; sparrows, finches, tits, thrushes, blackbirds, and starlings all gathered around, knowing instinctively that the big eagle would scorn to take them for food, while keeping away other predators such as cats and dogs. When she preened during her moult, feathers and down soft as cotton wool fell from her great body, and the little birds swooped down on the white flakes and carried them away to line their nests.

Atalanta looks suspiciously at a possible new friend

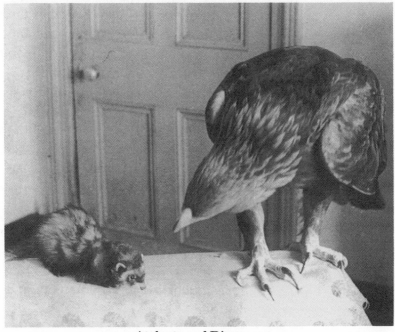

Atalanta and Diana

Yet the Pwllheli Council was always there, like a nagging tooth. Told he would be prosecuted without further notice if he persisted in encouraging Atalanta to fly for holiday makers, Sam decided on direct action.

On November 1, Sam and his friend Ron Semmens took Atalanta and drove to a Town Council meeting. A few hours earlier Sam had handed in a letter stating Atalanta's case, and he made sure the press knew that Atalanta would be a surprise visitor at the meeting.

The two men and the eagle waited in the anteroom until Sam decided to make a dramatic entry. He kicked the door open with such force that it crashed into a glass and wood partition and burst into the Council chamber with the largest golden eagle in the world on his shoulder. Seated at the horseshoe table were the surveyor, the treasurer, and the other Councillors, the town clerk, and the mayor. The men were all so startled that they had no time to compose themselves before Sam gave Atalanta's tail a smack, and her vast spreading wings seemed to fill the entire Council chamber.

Chaos broke out among the Councillors—they broke and ran. The press nearly slid under the table in laughter. The only man to remain seated was deaf old Tom Jones, who was nearly eighty and a friend of Atalanta's. He sat quietly, a grin on his face.

Sam shortened Atalanta's leash and she returned to his shoulder; Sam took her onto his fist and sat down while Atalanta preened herself indifferently.

Meanwhile the Council adjourned to an anteroom and the town clerk approached Sam.

"The Council wants you to take the eagle out again, Sammy, will you?"

"No."

"Please take her out for my sake, Sam. If you do your
points will be raised and the letter discussed."

"All right, Atalanta's done nothing." He paused and
added, "Go on, stroke her, Cyril."

The man stroked Atalanta, saying, "The Council can't
discuss anything with this whopping great bird at their
backs!"

Sam rose. "There's no legitimate complaint against my
bird. I brought her in to prove how harmless she is, and
now I want the complainants named."

Sam left as he had entered, the Berkut on his shoulder;
he parked her in the car, returning to the meeting alone.
The last item was "Correspondence and other business."
For this the Council spoke only in Welsh, so Sam did not
know what was said. Abruptly the mayor closed the meeting; as far as Sam knew, the promises he had been given had
gone for nothing and Atalanta had not been discussed. He
had been tricked. The next general meeting passed a reso-
lution to wipe out the complaints and petitions no one had
seen. Atalanta was free to fly but the abatement order was
still valid, although it could not be enforced unless Atalanta committed an offense.

The mystery remained, along with the identity of the
man who organized it. But by then Sam had much more serious concerns. Atalanta disappeared for twenty-nine days.

FIFTEEN

We have found peace, not your peace but the
eagles' peace as they hover, a terrible, bright,
unsure peace. . . . —HUMBERT WOLFE

IN the autumn of '65 Sam heard a rumor that a true Welsh polecat, a species sometimes said to be extinct, had been sighted in Cardiganshire near the Pant Glas Mountains. Sam decided to make the trip and, because he knew of her interest in animals, he made for Elma Williams' home at the foot of Pant Glas Mountain. He asked whether she had any polecats and was electrified by her reply.

"No, not polecats, but I have a golden eagle."

Sam could scarcely believe his ears. He badly wanted to mate Atalanta but did not believe there was a golden eagle in Wales, where no eagle had bred on Snowdon for more than two hundred years. The last female eagle had been shot as she brooded on her nest.

"An *eagle?*" he repeated in astonishment.

"Yes, a golden eagle. I call him the King. He objects to my bringing witnesses to his flight, but on most evenings I see him drifting against the sky. Inspector Heritage of the RSPCA has seen him planing about the valley; usually he flies with a retinue of seagulls, rooks, and other birds."

Just then a pair of buzzards passed overhead, mewing, and Sam's heart sank; buzzards and eagles look alike to the casual observer. Not wanting to sound disbelieving or rude, he said he had a golden eagle. "She's a Berkut, and the only one of her species in Europe. I very much want to mate her."

Elma glanced up at the sky. "I'm afraid my golden king isn't at home today. What a pity."

Sam was convinced of her sincerity, even allowing for her to be mistaken. "I'll bring Atalanta here and fly her for you," he said. "This is real eagle country, she'll like it."

He did not know at that time how very much she was going to like it!

A couple of weeks later Sam persuaded his friend Arnold to return with him to the Pant Glas area with Atalanta and Shep.

Elma gave the two men tea, and Sam was impatient to take Atalanta to the top of the hill and to release her so that she could enjoy such really splendid eagle country. He pulled on his gauntlet, Atalanta stepped readily onto it, and they were off. When they reached the top of the hill, he threw her up and she took off into the wind.

Watching her with proud eyes, Sam saw something that made him doubt his own vision. A second great eagle was silhouetted against the sky, soaring, planing—joining Atalanta! Then both great birds began their aerial acrobatics. This is a magnificent spectacle. Atalanta, a wild-caught bird, had all the powers of flight of the free born. In her Kirghiz days Sam had watched her superb flying with her mate, had seen her plummet out of the sun in a vertical swoop, spinning like a bullet from a rifled barrel at a speed of over 200 miles an hour, or take a tawny owl in a stoop, throw up to three hundred feet with the owl still in her talons, drop it, and see her companion eagle swoop under the falling owl, turn on its back, and catch it. Then the first eagle would bring the owl in at her master's whistle—this is one of the great sights of the world, greater still when the eagle is one's own bird.

Although several people watched the eagles' display, it was not, sad to say, photographed. The whole thing was entirely unexpected. Sam had taken Atalanta out simply for a pleasure flight, and then this incredible thing happened; he could hardly believe it himself. The only disappointment was that the stranger eagle was so large it seemed probable it was a female, not a possible mate for Atalanta. Sam decided that the strange female must have been on a migratory flight and had stopped to rest on the Pant Glas Mountain of Cardiganshire.

It was another two weeks before Sam could return again, but this time he took all his camera equipment. He put Atalanta on a rock on top of Pant Glas while the buzzards and seagulls and crows flocked above her. She took no notice but sat with the proud, aloof expression that belongs solely to the eagle family. Her splendid dark copper feathering seemed dusted with gold, especially across her shoulders.

Word of Atalanta's arrival got about, and many people followed them up the mountain to see her fly. Excitement rose, the crowd pressed about Atalanta, while Sam was busy setting up the cameras. This was not to Atalanta's liking, and before Sam realized what was happening, she took off— but without the bells he meant to fit before flying her. She did not use her wings to propel her down the mountain but glided, waiting, Sam knew, for his whistle to call her back. But in all the excitement, he had forgotten his whistle.

Atalanta sailed silently through the air without rising. In Sam's pocket her bells made muffled sounds, mocking him. Slowly, with heavy heart and no wish to discuss with the curious crowd what might have happened, he returned to the house and a search headquarters was set up. It was necessary to get full coverage from newspapers, radio, and television, so that Atalanta would not be shot at and, if sighted, her whereabouts would be relayed to Sam.

Shooting was stopped in the area; Atalanta did not lack for friends, chief among them Mr. Anderson, police officer of Talybont, and the RSPCA. Inspector Heritage of Aberystwyth motored many miles in bad weather searching for her. General Pugh, the high sheriff, had all his men on the lookout and he searched himself. His daughters actually saw Atalanta complete with her jesses, but they could not secure her. Nevertheless, at least Sam knew she was alive.

The telephone never stopped ringing; hundreds of people claimed to have seen her, but these calls always proved to be false. She was a will o' the wisp among those vast mountain ranges, where a few wingbeats in a strong blow could send her soaring fifty miles or more. Huntsmen, fishermen, gamekeepers, farmers, scouts, youth clubs, all helped in the search. The people of Cardiganshire and Montgomeryshire all joined in, all wanted to help.

Sam's friend Ron Semmens joined him. They spent many days searching for Sam's eagle in the mountains, often sleeping in the open in the rain, miles from anywhere, in a wilderness of jagged peaks and tangled undergrowth. Ron Semmens wrote: "I well remember one night that Sam and I spent in a thunderstorm, cramped in a telephone kiosk, God knows where. Then I had to pack it in, having ruined the gearbox in my car and believing myself that the search was hopeless. Sam, with his usual dogged determination, carried on searching, even though he too thought that by now Atalanta had probably crashed through the trees, her nine-foot wings unable to lift her from the tangle, and must be dead. He could only say, 'If I don't find her alive I'll find her dead, and there will be no mystery to taunt me.' "

Days went by; Sam was in despair. Elma drove Sam; they walked through miles of tough, precipitous mountainsides. They broadcast and followed every lead. It was no use.

During the brief periods when they returned to Elma's house, the telephone never ceased ringing. One day the phone rang, Elma answered it and handed it to Sam. His heart leaped.

It seemed that Atalanta had formed her own hunting range, taking in about sixty miles of wild, remote country jagged with mountains. She was living well on rabbits, hares, and foxes. Fantastic! Never before had a wild eagle been known to survive among hundreds of miles of rugged, mostly uninhabited mountains. It was the twenty-eighth day of the search; surely his luck must turn sometime.

He went on listening and was told that each evening Atalanta flew to a perch on a sheep wall on the mountain Brynuchel near Cwm-Llineau in Montgomeryshire. At the foot of the mountains in an old farmhouse lived the Evanses and their twelve children. Sam knew Atalanta's love of children and thought she might become lonely for human companionship. Sure enough, each day after school, five of the youngsters climbed the mountain "to play with the big eagle." They took their dog with them, and Atalanta played with the dog as she had with Shep at home in Pwllheli.

The children played with the bird for two weeks before anyone knew about it. On that fateful twenty-eighth day, a Sunday, the children's grandfather followed them up the mountain to see what they were up to.

The old man followed them quietly and watched them apparently waiting for something. Then he saw a huge eagle fly down to play with them. The old man went quickly down the mountain and tried to get the eldest boy to take the gun and shoot the bird before it harmed the children. Luckily the Evanses were good country folk with plenty of common sense. It was obvious that the bird must be someone's pet, although "pet" seemed a strange word to describe anything as fiercely splendid as Atalanta. Then they mentioned the leather jesses on her legs, and Mrs. Evans remembered reading about an escaped eagle from a Miss Williams' home and asked her husband to telephone there.

If it had not been for those children, Sam might never have found Atalanta. He investigated the story next day and decided this time it was true. Still there remained the question of catching her in all that rugged, mountainous country.

They left at dawn and it was dusk by the time they reached the farmhouse. Sam left Elma and set off himself with Meinir Wyn Jones, a thirteen-year-old, John Gwyn-da Evans, Gwynda Richards, and Geraint Evans. Without these children he could never have found the spot at the end of a ten-mile walk.

As darkness closed in, Sam became apprehensive that they would be unable to see the bird against the black, tangled undergrowth. On the other hand, eagles do not fly in darkness; besides, there was only a fifty-fifty chance of her coming anyway. They climbed along hard, stony, or bracken-covered slopes and crawled up rocky precipices.

Then Sam saw her. He sent the children back. He dared not risk his bird getting away from him in the dark. He knew that after twenty-eight days in the wild, she could no longer be the perfectly manned creature he knew. In fact, he thought it probable that she had reverted to the bird of prey she had been when he first took her.

He waited a few minutes to get his breath; the stiff climb following days and nights of anxiety was telling on him. Then he moved stealthily, slowly, nearer the eagle. All he could see was a formless black shadow like a rock, and it was as still.

Silently he reached out a hand, took her jesses, and held them firmly. Then he put the other hand around one great talon and jerked her onto his fist. She threw herself backward in a violent bate, crazy to escape. They fought it out, the Berkut and Sam, and it was not an easy battle. Throwing her great body up onto his weary arm, he turned and started down the mountain.

Sam was truly worn out from the weeks of searching; yet that night he walked more than ten miles with the massive bird on his fist. Again and again she bated, and he forced her back onto his fist, ignoring the fierce aching of his arm.

At last he felt that he was winning, and it was as well—he was almost exhausted as he stumbled over the cruel mountainside.

Somehow children, man, and eagle got back to the cottage. Sam was so weary he was almost drained of feeling. Atalanta was now sitting on his fist without bating, preening herself, the guest of honor and conscious of it. The children stroked her as Sam sat slumped in a chair, too tired to think; the only real thought in his mind was a dulled belief that persisted, telling him that his Berkut was happy to be loved and wanted once more.

After Mrs. Evans had given them all a meal and Sam had a short rest, he and Elma Williams drove off, Atalanta perched behind the driver and preening her hair. Back at Elma's, Atalanta jumped from the table and chair backs and onto his fist for her food. His joy was deep and strong as the realization grew that she remembered him and also remembered many of her lessons.

One thing about this new Atalanta puzzled him. A golden eagle at certain angles against the sun is black, but now the copper and gold that had feathered Atalanta a month before had disappeared; she had become a striking

Atalanta and friends

black, shining and glittering with a health unrealized by birds in captivity, however well cared for they may be. If he had first come upon Atalanta in broad daylight, Sam might have doubted her identity, even though he would have sworn he would know her in any feathering. This black Atalanta remained unknown and inexplicable: she was in truth *Die Schwarze Jägerine.*

It was only a couple of hours before the telephone began its incessant ringing. Photographers, film makers, and others arrived. Sam still had ahead of him the broadcasting studio at Aberystwyth.

One person visited was ninety-year-old General Ruck, brother of novelist Berta Ruck, who was very moved when he saw Atalanta, for she was by no means the first Berkut he had seen. At the turn of the century, General Ruck's regiment, the famous Bengal Lancers, were stationed on the Northwest Frontier, near the pass that had witnessed so much British gallantry. There he had hunted with a Berkut, and when the Pathans, those fierce fighting men of the hills, came on them during their hunts, they saw the Berkut and waved their rifles at them instead of shooting. A Berkut was as good as a passport among the wild tribesmen.

The telephone continued to ring. Teams of television experts were expected from London and from Germany, and reporters were everywhere. Sam considered the situation, then parked Atalanta in Elma Williams' car and, exhausted and feeling uncommonly cross, went to bed.

SIXTEEN

Nay if thou be that princely eagle's bird
Show thy descent by gazing 'gainst the sun. —SHAKESPEARE

THE *Western Mail* featured a front-page photograph and a long article on Atalanta and Sam. At home, film makers and reporters crowded the indifferent Atalanta, but Sam was still keyed up. He felt that no price was too high as long as he could look out of his window and see his eagle back home again, black and glossy now and happily playing on her lawn.

Two days after her return, Atalanta accomplished something unquestionably unique in the training of any hunting bird, a feat considered impossible by experts for any golden eagle, to say nothing of a Berkut, the most savage and intractable of its kind. Two days after her return from the wilderness, Sam and Atalanta spent three hours with a

Sam throws Atalanta up for a hunting foray © *John D. Drysdale*

television unit. A gale was blowing, and camera crews positioned themselves near to Atalanta's lawn while Sam flew her along the beach so she could make for her wall perch. The camera crew thought that they were being attacked by the Berkut and they scattered, cameras crashed, cameramen went backward over the promenade railings. It was all very funny to watch, but to Sam this was the hour of Atalanta's greatest triumph—never has any hawk, save Atalanta, lived wild for twenty-nine days and returned happily to her master. Most certainly no hawk in creation would, so soon after reclamation, have been able to accept all the confusion and fussing so characteristic of television cameras and crews.

Atalanta's month-long disappearance into the wild had had another, unforeseen consequence. The mystery man had grown bolder in his persecution of Atalanta, but the Pwllheli Council decided she had flown away and resolved only if she returned would they take steps under the Public Health Act. With her return, everyone was back to square one again.

One morning Sam opened the paper, and on the front page was a photograph of himself bringing Atalanta in to his fist as he stood on Pwllheli sands. The accompanying headline read:

WE'LL TAKE EAGLE

TO COURT

WARNS COUNCIL

Several months passed without further echoes of the newspaper heading. Then a man's name, neither a Welshman nor a local, began appearing in the local papers, accusing Atalanta of being a danger to children. Sam simply ignored this, although he could not help smiling to himself, for this man's daughter-in-law put her two-year-old son out in his pram in Atalanta's care. Atalanta would perch on the pram hood and guard the baby with fierce bright eyes and talons ready for any invader!

Atalanta resumed her regular flights. Sam wrote:

"It's Sunday, a beautiful sunny day. I'm dashing off a letter and then getting the hell out of here. Crowds pester me all day about Atalanta, and I want to go and sleep on a beautiful bird-rock seven miles from here, called Carreg-y-Llam. Thousands of breeding seabirds have arrived. Birds which spend their entire lives at sea are coming ashore to breed as they do once a year. I feel like having a lazy day, lulled to sleep by the music of their cries and around me the smell of spring flowers, fern, bracken, heather, and the sea."

It was Easter, 1969. "The best ever," Sam wrote. "I've worked fourteen birds this past winter. Atalanta is nest building, and it's a real mess-up. She's been trying to break a privet branch and she got her top mandible stuck in it, and I had to go and release her as she swung about screaming. Then she flew off with Shep after her and returned a few minutes ago with a baby rabbit no bigger than a rat, which she devoured. As I type she sits on the windowsill, watching me. . . ."

A few days later, "Atalanta is in the basement in disgrace. I've only fed her steak and a rabbit head for the last three days. Yesterday I was told she'd been hanging about our refuse pit, and last night she killed and ate a cheeky black-bird. She is very keen just now and I dare not give her a good crop of food. She brought up some rat fur in her casting this morning, and it can carry many types of disease. I've shut her indoors to stop any more hanky-panky."

Sam flew Atalanta so well and so often that he was able to watch the spectators even when flying her for their amusement. The watching faces invariably reflected wonder and excitement as he threw her into the wind. In typical flight she would take the wind with powerful wingbeats, find an up-draft until she hung, a great shining bird against an azure sky pierced by the mountain peaks of Lleyn and Snowdownia.

Shep ran beneath her, watching every move. Flocks of scavenging birds mobbed Atalanta; she ignored the birds above her, unless a gull or jackdaw rose in an attempt to join the throng above. There was power, arrogance, in the way the wary Atalanta tensed her wings and banked into a reckless stoop, legs extended, head lowered, hackles on end. Her feathering had returned to copper after its unnatural spell of darkness and her body gleamed in the sunshine, touched to gold as bright as her wing-covert feathers. One at a time the taloned feet flashed out: one foot struck at a gull while the second closed on a jackdaw, and she crushed both birds as easily as if they had been eggs. The mobbing birds had learned their lesson. Providing they kept above Atalanta they would be safe enough, even if they wanted to ride on her broad back.

The crowd watched her flight, clapping and shouting. Pwllheli is a small market town; it has to exist on its sum-

mer holiday trade. Atalanta earned her keep from everyone.

Sam took a magnificent action picture of Atalanta taking
a tawny owl while in flight, in a movement so swift it could
scarcely have been felt. In the picture it is possible to see
the way Atalanta beats her wings downward at the end of
her stoop to blanket the owl. Tawny owls, the largest of the
British species, are formidable foes. They will attack a man.
In the wild, hunting birds build an invisible wall around
their own range. They allow other birds to mob them, but
heaven help the bird of prey that penetrates that wall. Atalanta's prey was hunting on her own pitch, and Sam felt
sorry for the owl; he knew it must have young to be hunting in the daytime, but there was nothing he could do to
protect it. When Atalanta picked it out of the air, it turned
on its back and thrust out its talons to stab her, but she took
it without changing her flight pattern.

Sam has his worries when the air-sea helicopter comes
along the seafront. When he hears it, he rushes downstairs
because Atalanta seems to go mad; she attacks it while the
pilot tries to shoo her away. Sam is afraid the blades may hit
her.

That summer Sam took his eagle, his polecat, Diana, a
peregrine tiercel, and a prairie falcon, all chosen from his
fourteen trained birds, to a German wine festival. In a letter from Germany he wrote, "The peregrine tiercel has
done well; the prairie falcon, damn it, keeps waiting-on too
low, and if I fly her at *nabelkrahen* (hooded crows) she is
not really high enough for one effective stoop, and we have
to follow the damn thing because she chases after her prey.

Atalanta's made a tremendous impression in the Steinadler section, she is much bigger than the German, Austrian, Bavarian, or French eagles.

"As for me, you once called me 'the finest falconer,' but I am not. I'm only too conscious of being just an amateur. My friend, Dr. Saar, is the best Western European falconer. I'm not thorough. I do not train for a particular flight at specially chosen prey. I disobey the rules and am unmethodical. I fly birds for fun and relaxation. I want to understand their instincts, the brains beneath the feathers. Competition does not worry me. I go to meet fellow falconers, to learn from them, drink with them, enjoy their company; they are a breed apart. They have strange superstitions. One falconer never wishes another falconer 'good luck'; instead you wish the bird will foul on the falconer's back!"

Summer had been ushered in with all the violence of a capricious spring—with gales, mist, and winds. One day, Sam swam out in the freezing sea with Atalanta on his fist and Shep swimming beside him, unaided by the shots of corn whiskey which bore Sam up. He threw Atalanta up and brought her in onto his bare arm, a feat never before accomplished by anyone with an eagle, and came out of the sea claiming he never felt a thing!

Sam wrote, "Atalanta is in tremendous yarak. I don't understand it, I can't tire her. She will be very late before her moult finishes this year; she will sicken immediately she does start. It must be the cold weather; the plants, fish, trees, and seabirds are also late this year.

"Have just measured Atalanta, forty-two and a half

inches from beak to tail tip. She is full of life, soaring above the mobbing birds following her. In this tremendous yarak she's being fed each day. It's her hunting season and she's chasing and tearing up everything in sight, including the towels and cushions from my sun divan on the lawn. She's reached the stage when I've seen her go for bulls, and she attacks the helicopter!"

It was June 30, 1969, the night before the investiture of Charles of England as Prince of Wales.

SEVENTEEN

. . . it is a thievish form of hunting to shoote gunnes and bows, and grey-hound hunting is not so martial a game. —KING JAMES I ADVICE TO HIS SON ON BECOMING PRINCE OF WALES.

THE landlord of the Llanaelhaiarn pub saw Atalanta chasing a fox on one of the Rival Mountains on the eve of the July 1 investiture. Later she was seen eating prey on Bardsey Island, said to be the burial place of twenty thousand saints and a sanctuary for migrating birds, which until recently had its own King Pritchard. By early evening she had flown home to her lawn at Wave Crest, preening herself for a large audience of holiday makers and visitors for the investiture the next day at Caernarvon Castle, a few miles away.

Sam took Shep for his usual midnight run on the beach, and when he arrived home Atalanta was perched on her window ledge. He followed the nightly ritual of tickling her keel while Atalanta fluffed her breast feathers and clucked contentedly.

It was a dark night with heavy overclouding, and Sam looked out through his bedroom window before falling asleep. Some time after 2 P.M. he woke to the frightened growling of Shep, on guard at Sam's bedroom door.

Suddenly the bedroom seemed to be filled with fire, and a rumble like delayed thunder roared out across the sea. A bomb set the sky aflame in blazing red and white light. Sam sprang out of bed and ran to the window.

On the lawn below, Atalanta appeared to have gone mad, crashing into object after object, attempting to get airborne. The lawn was littered with her feathers, many of them new, still in the blood, for she was moulting. Heartbroken at the sight of her destroying herself in her terror, Sam ran, naked as he was, downstairs.

By the time he reached the lawn, Atalanta had somehow become airborne in spite of her intense fear and was disappearing across the promenade toward the beach and the sea. The blazing glow in the sky was fading. Atalanta, a black moving blot, changed to a dot and was lost in the distance.

Sam rushed back to his bedroom, pulled on trousers and sweater, and raced back with Shep at his heels. Still in darkness, Sam and Shep crossed the Parade to the beach and then went across the sand dunes. Shep quartered the ground in front of him; it was dangerous walking in the blackness of night with Sam clambering among rocks and on the precipitous cliffs. Dawn broke and he raised his binoculars.

There was no sign of Atalanta. Years of studying bird life

in the mountains has given Sam a sensitive, built-in ability to think almost like a bird. He felt certain that Atalanta would head straight into the wind through the darkness and not rise and ride the thermals as she usually did in the daytime. At a few thousand feet a thermal can be as fast as a hundred and forty knots, so it was as well she was unlikely to do this at night, unless fear changed the whole pattern of her flight.

It was 7:30 in the morning when Sam paused and lifted his head wearily. He heard excited barking from Shep and began running over the star-grass covered dunes. There among the high coarse grass stood the piteously frightened Atalanta, all her hackle feathers raised in defiance. She was highly dangerous when in that state; she ran stabbing at Shep with her talons. Sam settled down to soothing and coaxing her. Finally he persuaded her to step onto his fist. As he turned to carry her the four and a half miles home, Atalanta took off and she flew half a mile before she landed again on the sand dunes. Sam could see the damage to her wings; big gaps and bloodstains showed where the feathers had been torn out.

More patience, more stalking, and the weary Sam coaxed her onto his fist. He fastened her jesses swiftly and drew her legs tightly onto his double-strength buffalo-hide falconry glove. This was the preliminary to a battle royal.

Atalanta fought against returning to her lawns where this terrible thing had happened to her; but she could not escape, although she could and did inflict terrible punishment on Sam, who understood that this violence came from her fear, not viciousness. Now as he carried her she developed a frenzy of fear, gripping his arm with her right talons. Sam gasped in agony; her talons pierced the gauntlet and went through his arm and into his elbow bone. Both were exhausted long before Sam carried her through the home gate. Putting her in a blacked-out room in the basement, he left to get an antitetanus injection. He had to carry his arm in a sling for three days.

Poor Atalanta, she made a slow recovery from the petrol bomb used by the Welsh extremists to burn down a large marquee nearby erected by the sailing club, whose members had arranged a barbecue to celebrate the investiture. In spite of warships and submarines in Cardigan Bay and soldiers, tanks, armored cars, and police on watch everywhere, senseless fires took place all over the principality.

Sam was bitterly upset by Atalanta's injuries. Where the feathers had been torn from her wings, Sam sealed the holes. It was a week before he attempted to put her out on her lawn. When he did, she went crazy again, and he had to settle down and begin her training right from the beginning for the third time and with a useless left arm.

Three months later, although Atalanta's feathers were growing, her wings gave her great pain if she attempted to rouse. Luckily she could fly, and she was at home on her own lawn again with her temper apparently unspoiled. She played all day with Shep, but every night Sam took her down to the basement mews. She flew only under careful control, and Sam decided to keep her to this regime until she would be hard-penned sometime in late November or December.

Sam suffered some of Atalanta's pain to see her in her un-

stable, fear-induced condition, and with so many ruthlessly torn-out feather shafts.

In August he wrote, on his return from sailing a ketch round the coast to capture an Irish peregrine, "I've had Atalanta with me every minute in a special traveling crate to which she is now accustomed. As you know, one mistake and a hunting bird can be finished. Atalanta damaged herself badly when the bomb went off, she tore out many feathers that were still in the blood. She's still dangerous to handle; she can fly, but not with any power. It will be November before the seconds grow and become hard-penned in her right wing. I won't fly her at prey until it is all right."

In September Sam's letters emphasized Atalanta's slow progress. "It is pitiful to see the state of her wings. Heaven knows when she'll be ready again for game. Her temper is improving, she's so pleased to be home that she is playing all over her lawn as I write, and I've had to bring Shep in out of her way. Sadly, Atalanta killed and ate a white duck, so I've hand fed her every day since, and there's been no repetition."

A week later he wrote, "Atalanta has moulted well on her body, her wings are a mess, they must pain her a lot because she flies into tempers and is very dangerous, even with me. I shut her up at night now. She killed two dogs that strayed onto her lawn one day, and even Shep gives her a wide berth. Yesterday they had a hell of a fight, but Shep knows how to tackle and worry her. It will be late November or December before she is feather perfect. Ordinarily she would be hunting now; she is in physical condition but without having the proper powers of flight. Boy, you should see the breadth of her, she's like a bull. Right now she's perched on the window ledge, swiveling her head about. Fantastic how she picks up every movement in the sky.

"My little bird friends are all around me pinching my nasturtium seeds which I meant to pick and plant again next year, and Atalanta is obviously wondering if it would be wasted effort to chase them."

A month later Sam's anxiety was still apparent. "Atalanta is outside with a crop full of raw eggs, steak, and chicken. I won't fly her for weeks yet. She can jump from perch to perch and extend her wings, but it hurts her to attempt to exercise them. The new feathers are sore as teeth. She screams if I attempt to break the hard ends of the sheaths, but if I don't they will mark the inside webbing like fretted hunger marks. Luckily she appears all right anatomically; I've never before had her like this in September. I hand feed her to be sure she gets all her vitamins and does not get marked by blood, which attracts the flies. Every day I spray her with a stirrup pump and she dries in the wind and the sun. A few weeks ago the mayor of London came to see her; but I am only aching to see her soaring aloft again."

In November he wrote, "Atalanta will wait another six weeks before I try her out with hard flying. She just came flying like hell onto the window ledge when a shower started, and when I wouldn't let her in she flew back and tore up her padded perch. The blighter wants to attract my attention, and she's trying to attack Shep who is inside with me. There is one retrice feather in her tail and a number in her left wing to get right still, and she is dangerous at present, even in play. God, she is lovely . . . two feathers enclosed from Atalanta who is now perched on a garden post. One is a lanceolate feather tipped in gold, from her nape. These are the feathers that give the species their name of golden eagle. Fantastic things, feathers, thousands of tiny hooklets holding the filaments. . . ."

Finally, in January, 1970, "Atalanta's plumage is magnificent, but one wing is by no means normal."

Correct landing technique—note balance

EIGHTEEN

And she was a golden lily in the dew,
And she was as sweet as an apple on the tree
And she was as fine as a melon in the corn-field,
Gliding and lovely as a ship on the sea.

—VACHEL LINDSAY

GRADUALLY Atalanta, strong, well cared for, and a creature of the seasons, became more her old self. After many months, her wing recovered so that Sam could fly her again.

In early spring Atalanta dropped the second feathering from her left wing. This worried Sam because during her moult she needs extra blood for her new feathers; this can impair her strength and flying ability. The next day the second feather finger in her right wing fell, and the down from her body lay on the lawn like snowflakes.

One afternoon Atalanta spotted a hare eating grass by the roadside. Sam watched Atalanta; she reacted like an athlete loosening up, setting herself tensely on half-open wings, the shoulders of the splendid wings rounded and heavy with bone and muscle, like the carapace of muscle on a boxer.

Atalanta went on to do knee bends, as if about to take off from her tall, concrete perch. She shifted her eyes, her head bobbed up and down and turned from side to side, as she judged the distance to the hare. Taking off in a low flight across the roadway and over the beach, she banked sideways into the wind, gave a few strong wingbeats, and then flew straight for the hare in a calculated maneuver aimed at preventing it from jinking into the cover of star grass.

The unsuspecting hare continued browsing as Atalanta flew low and fast; her wings whipped the air with a whistling sound. Suddenly the hare sat up, ears erect, then in panic it bounded off. Atalanta had the hare right where she wanted it, and it looked as if the unfortunate creature had made a suicidal maneuver; the eagle was already falling in her death dive. She splayed her tail and her backpedaling wings broke her speed, her talons relaxed in readiness to circle the chest of the racing hare in a viselike grip.

Sam saw the sand swirl up from the roadway; the hare jumped a full ten feet over the patch of bramble and disappeared among the sand dunes! The bewildered Atalanta bounced on her legs, ran a few paces to get airborne again, and then circled slowly away to return home a few minutes later with a large sprig of heather in her beak.

Atalanta had missed her strike by more than a foot, a sure sign that her moult had really started. But if Sam was distressed by her error of judgment, Atalanta had more important things on her mind. She had decided to begin to nest.

In the wild, golden eagles nest on cliffs, occasionally in trees. The nest is made of sticks, dry grasses, and moss. Usually two large, nearly round eggs, white or blotched with chestnut or red, are laid at intervals of three or four days. Incubation takes six or seven weeks. The young are fed on the nest for about eleven weeks, during which time the male provides most of the food. The nestlings go through three stages, all of which are white; they reach adult plumage in the third or fourth year. Allowing for the differences in terrain and in the type of prey, golden eagles remain golden eagles. Sam's aim with Atalanta was to satisfy her instincts with a life that was as nearly normal as possible.

In her wild state her mate would already have built the nest; and then, while Atalanta was egg-laying and brooding, he would have been hunting to feed her. With the loss of most of her flight powers, she would concentrate on the task of laying, brooding, and looking after her chicks.

During this time Atalanta's temperament changed completely.

The beautiful eagle was a hopelessly inept nestmaker. She showed an especial fondness for Sam and put on an air of great solicitude while he made a solid foundation for the side of the nest. She "talked," clucking and kek-kek-kek-king, and insisted that Sam should fuss over her all day long. Even her friend Shep, toward whom she was so often bossily playful, was now treated with docility. Suddenly she became very docile, very loving toward everything and everybody. For the next few weeks she hardly flew at all, merely launching herself for short flights if a very strong southwesterly was blowing. Except for taking an occasional young rabbit, she hunted no other game, and Sam provided an endless supply of chicken heads, necks, livers, hearts, yolks of eggs, and red meat—hares and rabbits. He also made sure that she had sticks, heather branches, fur pelts, brushwood, hay, turf, and moss in plenty, so that she would have a wide choice of materials for her nest. She decided that the best place for her nest was between two concrete blocks in the shelter of the hedge.

Sam wrote, "Atalanta played and fussed for half an hour at a time, clucking to herself as she carried a twig about, either in her beak or clutched in her foot, before placing it. She never put sticks in the right places, often placing them where they were not even near to the nest." So Sam set to and built the whole nest for her. He lined it with red velvet, which gave it a distinctly regal appearance, and saw to it that the nest was large enough for the golden bird to have plenty of room and complete peace and comfort for the important business of egg-laying.

One morning in mid-March Sam looked through his bedroom window and saw Atalanta suddenly hurl herself from the nest to chase poor old Shep viciously round and round the lawn, until he finally had to jump over the wall to escape her. The poor old chap was so frightened by this change in his recently solicitous friend that he ran across the road and on to the promenade before, in answer to Sam's whistle, he tried to return to the lawn. Atalanta went quite berserk and rushed at him again. Once more Shep hurled himself over the fence and stood panting, pleading for his master not to order him back again.

Thoroughly puzzled by the eagle's change of heart, Sam

approached Atalanta, who had already returned to her nest. Her hackles rose warningly, telling Sam to keep his distance. When he took no notice of the warning, the great bird rushed at him, stabbing at his legs and screaming with rage. Sam was so busy dodging her attacks that it was some time before he noticed the large, mottled white egg in the nest.

Poor Atalanta, in her own eyes she was a mother protecting her egg. Her entire attitude to the world had changed. Once again she was the fierce copper killer of the mountain crags, ready to attack and kill anything or anyone who dared to come between her and her precious egg.

Sam beat a hasty retreat, but he was overjoyed; after her many tribulations and changes, she had proved she still had her instinct and her ability to brood.

Two days later another egg appeared on the red velvet nest lining. By now the eagle and her master had reached a compromise. Atalanta was speaking to him again, twittering and clucking as he approached her, lifting her splendid head to nibble round his wristwatch as he held one hand out to her, reaching under her with the other to examine what he knew, sadly, must be two infertile eggs.

As Sam peered at Atalanta's eggs, she roused her feathers, puffing them out in her own absurd way, clucking and kekking like any bloody old hen. Sam replaced the eggs and Atalanta opened up her breast feathers and covered them with the warmth of her high-temperatured body, brooding them lovingly. From then on, whenever Sam thought she needed exercise, she kept the nest under constant observation during her flight, soaring level with the roofs of the

"Atalanta is nest building, and it's a real mess-up."

Atalanta's nurseling

Infertile eggs

houses. And if he pretended to go indoors, Atalanta came down in a flash, determined to guard and keep warm the two eggs Sam knew could never hatch.

Atalanta's love for these two beautiful, useless eggs was so touching that Sam and his friends puzzled over what they might do for her. Someone suggested he should go to Scotland to find two fertile Scottish golden eagle eggs with which to replace Atalanta's. Sam decided against this. For one thing he would be breaking the law, although this was a minor worry because, if taken fresh, the Scottish eagle would lay again. But most of the Scottish eggs were infertile from man's use of pesticides; and the species of eagle was smaller and lighter in color than the great Berkut. The chances of a successful exchange did not seem worthwhile to Sam.

Atalanta's devotion to her brooding became daily more pitiful to her master. Day in, day out, she warmed the two rotting eggs while Sam looked after her as a male eagle would have, feeding her, guarding her eggs while she took her exercise flights.

Sam wondered how long it would be before Atalanta's instinct told her to abandon her eggs; as yet, she showed no signs of frustration. In spite of their infertility, the eggs were warmed and guarded beneath her body day and night, in rain or sunshine. She settled herself on them by rolling them over with her beak, then she raised her breast high, opened the feathers down the center of her body, and folded herself down so that she enclosed the eggs like a feathery cloak warmed by the high temperature of her body.

All this loving care was doomed to failure. Sam watched his great savage bird with increasing compassion, saw her landing with dry sticks in her beak to add to the nest beneath the privet hedge. This always started a to-do that ended by her putting the stick in some useless place, then returning to the nest, kek-kekking softly to the chicks she would never have. She would walk around within the nest in circles and come to attention clenching her talons like closed fists, using infinite care not to pierce the precious, brittle-shelled things before she setttled down to brood them.

Late one evening Sam stopped his car near the river at Bodegroes estate so that he could watch four baby otters at play. Sam tries very hard to enforce the protection of otters; he is puzzled by the Celts' lyricism, on the one hand, and their barbaric pleasure in killing their own exclusive, almost extinct, otters, on the other. Because of their lack of compassion, there are now only seven holts left in all Caernarvonshire.

Thus it gave Sam special joy to see the sleek little otters playing so happily. He gave them chicken heads and giblets and was sitting there watching them eat their supper, when he heard a noise like a saw cutting through a tough tree trunk. This was followed by the cry of an adult tawny owl from a nearby tree.

Sam walked to the base of the tree and looked down at a white puffball of fluff that was snapping its little beak at him; the sawing sound had been the fallen chick calling for its mother. Sam stooped, lifted the baby, and began climbing up the tree to return it to the nest hole, when a thought struck him. He climbed down, still holding the baby owl, and drove home with it. He filled its crop with soft red meat dipped in egg yolk and put it overnight in a parrot cage.

Next morning he rose at dawn, put the beak-cracking powder puff in his pocket, and went out to Atalanta. She was very reluctant to leave her eggs. Twice when he took her up, she left his fist and flew onto one of her perches. Finally he managed to throw her up for an exercise flight.

As soon as she disappeared, Sam substituted the tiny tawny owlet for one of the eggs. Then, with bated breath, he watched for the eagle's return, wondering anxiously if she would consider the little one as a nestling or breakfast. Sam dreaded harm coming to the fluffy infant owl.

Atalanta landed on her lawn perch. She took a moment to look about her, then jumped off the perch and waddled across the lawn to her nest. She heaved herself over the side of the nest and paused, gazing puzzled at her changeling. Then the piercing stare took on the look of a child discovering a new toy. The baby owl made cracking noises of defiance as it gazed up at its large new mother.

Atalanta's pathetic attempts at mothering the little thing were touchingly comic. The awesome beak tried to preen the fluffy ball before her, and the owl's tiny beak snapped at the eagle. Then there was a moment of marvelous comedy. The baby owl flopped out of the nest, and Atalanta, like some ridiculous clown, fell backward into the privet!

Sam replaced the owlet and fed it with small pieces of meat, while Atalanta recovered her balance, clucked, and watched the feeding performance in amazement. Then she settled herself on the remaining addled egg, and the baby owl, full of nourishment and spirit, jumped all around and over her, smacking the great hunting bird with its downy wings and upsetting her so, that finally Atalanta had to extend a wing and guide the baby beneath it with her beak. Even then the small owl would not keep still. As Sam went indoors to have his breakfast, poor Atalanta sat rocking back and forth in her efforts to control her willful baby.

After breakfast Sam returned to find the situation changed. Atalanta had settled down over the softness of her foster infant, and she refused to move when Sam went and offered her a ration of raw meat. Ordinarily Atalanta craved bone and fur, but now she could think of nothing but her new baby. She only wanted her baby to sleep on undisturbed while she brooded over it. Poor Atalanta, her soft underparts were sore and worn almost bare of feathers because of the unnaturally prolonged sitting over the two hard-shelled eggs.

Now that things seemed to be going well, Sam returned to the tawny owl's nest and took another baby to substitute for the second infertile egg. Atalanta made no protest; she simply settled down over the two downy, drowsy infants, and she never moved until dusk began to fall.

Evening, had Atalanta known it, was the crux of the whole affair. Owls, being nocturnal, will drowse through the day, especially if they have been well fed, but darkness brings to life the instincts that are common to all night hunters and feeders. At dusk both babies came to vigorous life, and they began to give their foster mother a very difficult time.

The big mother was gently solicitous as, with Sam's help, she tore the meat into small pieces and fed them. But the little owls became tiny poltergeists of the night; they delighted in scrambling out of the nest, flapping, and running about. Sam made a hurriedly constructed fence of wire netting around the nest. This helped to give Atalanta more time to puzzle out how she could fend for them.

It was a great problem; as darkness fell, the little ones began their vigorous life—just at the time when all Atalanta's instincts told her to sleep. How to combine the opposing natures of owl and eagle? By morning Atalanta was glad to be flown as a respite from the two restless babies. She took the air, soaring, gliding, she snap-rolled, dived, and swooped out over the sea, and for the first time in weeks she seemed to find her old exhilaration in flight.

After she had been in the air for an hour, she came down and bathed; then dripping with water, she spread herself out in the cold sunshine and the breeze to dry like a tousled bunch of copper chrysanthemums. Meanwhile Sam had fed the owlets and they were flapping about their wire enclosure.

When she was almost dry, Atalanta jumped over the wire and stepped onto her nest, attempting to settle over her babies. It was an impossible task. One little owl was docile enough, and she soon guided it under a protective wing. It seemed to accept its new mother.

The second nestling was a different proposition altogether. As Atalanta attempted to push it near to the warmth of her body, the small owl threw itself on its back as a kitten will and sank its needle-sharp talons into Atalanta's face. Small and fluffy as it appeared to be, owlets are very strong; its talons could have blinded Atalanta as they pierced her face around the cere and the eye. The eagle screamed with pain; ruffling her feathers, she flashed out her foot to drag off the small demon that had attacked her and would not loosen its grip on her face.

Had Atalanta wished, she could have destroyed the owlet with one squeeze of her powerful talons; but she did not. Sam somehow managed to make the owl loosen its grip and, as he struggled, the great Berkut lived up to her reputation for ferocity. Blinded by pain, she tore part of the nest asunder and aimed deadly blows at Sam with a lightning quickness. He used his gauntlet to protect one arm as he tried to pull the baby away with his free hand. The baby loosened its hold and Atalanta reared back to recover.

That settled the question of what was going to happen to the mischievous owlet. A half hour later Sam returned it to its family in the tree hole nest at Bodegroes. It had suffered little from its boldness to its foster mother; it was a very lucky baby owl to be alive at all.

When Sam returned home from rehousing the baby owl, he was rather surprised to find Atalanta sunning herself and preening the remaining owlet, which had settled contentedly at her side. It was obviously well fed, for its tiny crop bulged. Mother eagle and baby owl had both come over the netting enclosure, and dozens of spectators stood by the garden wall to watch as the eagle rubbed her feathers with oil from her preen gland, dabbing at it with her beak. From time to time she ran her great shining beak proudly up and down the owlet's downy plumage like a mother settling her child's hair. Sam looked at his bird's penetrating eyes under the frowning brows and thought what an amazing bird she was, so proud, so lovely, and so loving.

Sam soon removed the wire netting barricade so that mother and nestling could have more freedom. Every night was a wearying time for Atalanta. Her nocturnal baby screeched so persistently and loudly that some neighbors complained. As a compromise, Sam took the baby each evening and put it in the parrot cage on the coal shed roof. To his astonishment, every night brought with it the silent, muffled flight of the parent owls to feed their baby!

At daybreak, Sam returned the baby to Atalanta on the front lawn. Soon the little one began to lose her down and the feathers came through. Like all owls, the baby drowsed all day long, but it ate well from its daily supplement of soft foods such as liver, heart, soft meat, and kidney. All day Atalanta followed it, studying her foster baby's strange routines and half-asleep activities. These deviations from what she might have expected appeared to surprise her; but for hours the two would share the largest wooden perch on the lawn, sitting side by side, the baby snuggling close to Atalanta's great wing.

After a time, as its feathers grew and it became hard-penned, the owlet flew short distances. Each night the owlet returned to the parrot cage at the back of the house where its true parents brought it a variety of foods, which amazed Sam.

Late one evening, after the owlet was able to tear its own food, Sam listened for the answering call of the parent birds. He put a red rubber ring on the young owl's leg for

identification, then opened the cage door and went indoors
to watch what would happen.

It was almost dusk when the owlet flew out of the cage
and landed on a goalpost of the nearby Pwllheli football
ground. Minutes later it was joined by an adult tawny owl.
He watched them until it was too dark to see the goalposts
any longer; the two owls were still perched there.

Sam had deliberately taken the owlet from Atalanta before it had flown free. In the wild state, a young eaglet is
driven ruthlessly away from its parents as soon as it can
fend for itself. The parents may force it to wander thousands of miles before it reaches maturity, finds a mate of its
own, and settles down. Atalanta was moulting strongly; obviously the baby owl did not require her protection any
longer. Knowing Atalanta's nature, Sam reasoned that if
the eagle attempted to drive away her foster child when she
found it a bore, she might inadvertently kill it. So to avoid
an unhappy ending, Sam separated the owl from the eagle,
knowing that the owlet would soon adjust to life with its
parents.

It did become necessary for Sam to identify the young
owl; soon after he released it, it was hit by a car. The owl
was brought to Sam in a dazed condition. Once again luck
was with Atalanta's nurseling, and the next evening Sam
threw the recovered bird from his bedroom window. Silently as death, the soft-feathered owl flew off and disappeared.

Even without her nurseling, Atalanta had enough
problems. She had a bad time with her moult, and Sam
wanted her feather perfect for the autumn. Atalanta's time
of loving gentleness had come and gone. There was the sure

knowledge that it would return but, Sam reflected sadly, in her case it would mean only other infertile eggs on which she would lavish her love. It was a tragic waste; he wished wholeheartedly that he could get her a mate. Without a mate there would be no more Atalantas, no more great birds "gorgeous as the sun in midsummer," and this would be a poorer world.

It seemed impractical for Sam to go on another expedition to try to find a mate for Atalanta. But as time went on, he knew it was the only way, especially when he learned that there were soon to be new laws concerning the importation of birds, strict laws that would add to the difficulty of the task.

One serious problem for Sam was the fact his eagle was a one-man bird. He had only to recall the way Atalanta had behaved when he had been forced to leave her with his friends Griff Thomas and Ron Semmens, who knew her well and sometimes handled her. On the first occasion when Sam was absent, Griff Thomas visited Atalanta late in the evening. For weeks he had been able to stroke her head and she had flown free to his baited fist. So that night, full of hope, he went to her mews and peered through the shadows to find her on one of her perches. He reached out his hand to stroke her. Atalanta's hackles rose, she clenched her talons ready to stab him, and delivered a warning peck.

Next day he visited the lonely eagle earlier in the day. She had enjoyed her morning bath, but after that she became obviously more and more miserable, staring continuously before her with her dark, brooding eyes, waiting in vain for her master.

Griff Thomas put on the gauntlet and offered her some

meat. She turned away. He dangled the meat before her beak and eventually, despairing of her taking it, he put it on the block at her feet. She bent her head, picked it up, and dropped it onto the grass. As he moved around her, stroking the back of her head, she swiveled to face him, ready to peck. So much for one of Atalanta's most successful handlers. Ron Semmens had much the same experience. Atalanta is fine with Sam's friends, just as long as he is there with them.

On another occasion Sam had to be away for ten days. After three days neither of his two friends dared open Atalanta's mews' door to feed her. Sam had filled a bath for her and had fed her with eggs, steak, and chicken before he left, so ten days without food would do her no harm, but he hated to think of her prolonged loneliness and deep misery. There is little Sam can do for Atalanta if he has to leave her for more than three days; he can only put her on a long tether in her basement mews, because no one can handle her after that time and her food has to be thrown to her. This, perhaps more than all the difficulties of crossing borders to reach the region where he might expect to find her a mate, made Sam reluctant to consider the prospect of an expedition.

Nevertheless, slowly Sam forced himself to face facts. Too many years have gone by for Shep, he can no longer hunt well over the magic Welsh mountains after the speeding shadow of Atalanta. Now only Atalanta throws the pointed shadows of her wings across the bitter hillsides, on Cader Idris, the place of eagles, while she waits for her "season of mist and mellow fruitfulness" and for the shadows of other wings in pursuit of her own.

EPILOGUE

ONCE again a tall, blond man, with the look of a raffish Danny Kaye, gazes across the flat land of a small airstrip between Europe and Asia. Sam's hair is covered by a fur-lined, ear-flapped ski hat. His stockings are stuffed into cleated mountain boots. He wears his heavy sheepskin jacket that he says "stinks like a slaughterhouse when it rains." At his feet a bulging rucksack holds the extra-large, brilliant red wind-cheater he will wear over everything so that any companions will see him at a distance. It also holds a brandy flask and hard sweets to suck, both of which he will need at high altitudes, sunglasses that are slitted wooden discs to wear against snowglare and bad weather, an ice pick, and oxygen mask and cylinders for the great heights—the minimum a man needs for such an adventure. So far so good. That is the outward man.

Inwardly Sam is exhausted by the effort to make the decision to leave Atalanta for the shortest time possible—three, at most four, weeks—in which to get her a mate. Sam is a gambler, but he came to this decision only after making every possible provision for her protection and care, and he knows there still remains an element of chance.

He has worked out the maximum time he can allow to reach the snows of Tien Shan, to capture, willy-nilly, a mate for Atalanta, and to return. He knows the safety limit of her fasting, and he believes he can keep his journey within that limit. It is the possibility of delay that frightens him, delay through political interference, accident, the actual acquiring of the eagle whether he goes it alone or faces the Easterners' bargaining that he knows from experience can be so impossibly prolonged. In that case he will return and his trip will be for nothing.

With luck, the lift he now awaits will take him across the border and some hundreds of miles on his journey to where the next to the last stage will be by yak, and then to the final stage, which will require all his mountaineering skill. As he watches for the plane to appear against the leaden sky, he thinks anxiously of Atalanta, whose need for a mate has finally sent him to find one for her. A precious two days have gone by; his worried mind is back in Wales—another day and Atalanta's need for her master will make her savage; she will be unpredictable, too, from a natural hunger which she refuses to satisfy.

Sam looks again at the horizon and the heavy sky as a

faint vibration touches his ears. The craft appears in the distance, casting no shadow because of the heavy overcast. The cold sky recedes. In its place he sees the snowy peaks of Tien Shan rising against ice-blue skies, the snowfields lit by pale sunlight. He does not watch the advancing plane because his mind's eye is filled by the image of a great-winged Berkut coming out of the eye of the sun, stooping in a path of flame—a hunting bird, fit mate for the eagle awaiting him. He is a big bird for a male, this bird of Sam's imagination, a deadly concentration of power and controlled nerves and muscles giving to the elastic strength of the wind. Suddenly his ten thousand wing muscles cease to fight the air and go into a controlled collapse that makes him part of his element. . . . Sam's imagination turns homeward to fertile eggs, the soft kek-kekking, the mother's warmth and love; eaglets sleeping through the night, growing mightily on plentiful food, wing-flapping through the day as their magnificent mother guards them; and then the release of the two hunters and the enjoyment of what Markham, in 1615, called "a most princely and serious delight."

The air is filled with sound. Sam reaches down and lifts his heavy rucksack onto his shoulders. He walks to the gate to see his transport touch down. He is on his way.

Bird of Jove
© *Bob Bird*